Ada Meadows
Sept 4, 1920

PEKING DUST

Loading coolies at Wei-Hei-Wei

PEKING DUST

BY

ELLEN N. LaMOTTE

Author of "The Backwash of War"

ILLUSTRATED
WITH PHOTOGRAPHS

NEW YORK
THE CENTURY CO.
1919

Published, May, 1919

INTRODUCTION

Two classes of books are written about China by two classes of people. There are books written by people who have spent the night in China, as it were, superficial and amusing, full of the tinkling of temple bells; and there are other books written by people who have spent years in China and who know it well,—ponderous books, full of absolute information, heavy and unreadable. Books of the first class get one nowhere. They are delightful and entertaining, but one feels their irresponsible authorship. Books of the second class get one nowhere, for one cannot read them; they are too didactic and dull. The only people who might read them do not read them, for they also are possessed of deep, fundamental knowledge of China, and their views agree in no slightest particular with the views set forth by the learned scholars and theorists.

This book falls into neither of these two classes, except perhaps in the irresponsibility of its author. It is compounded of gossip, —the flying gossip or dust of Peking. Take it lightly; blow off such dust as may happen to stick to you. For authentic information turn to the heavy volumes written by the acknowledged students of international politics.

ELLEN N. LA MOTTE.

ACKNOWLEDGMENT

The writer wishes to thank the folfowing friends who have been kind enough to lend the photographs used in the illustrations: Warren R. Austin, F. C. Hitchcock, Margaret Frieder, T. Severin and Rachel Snow.

CONTENTS

PART I

Letters Written October and November, 1916

PART II

Letters Written February and March, 1917

CONTENTS

LIST OF ILLUSTRATIONS

PART I

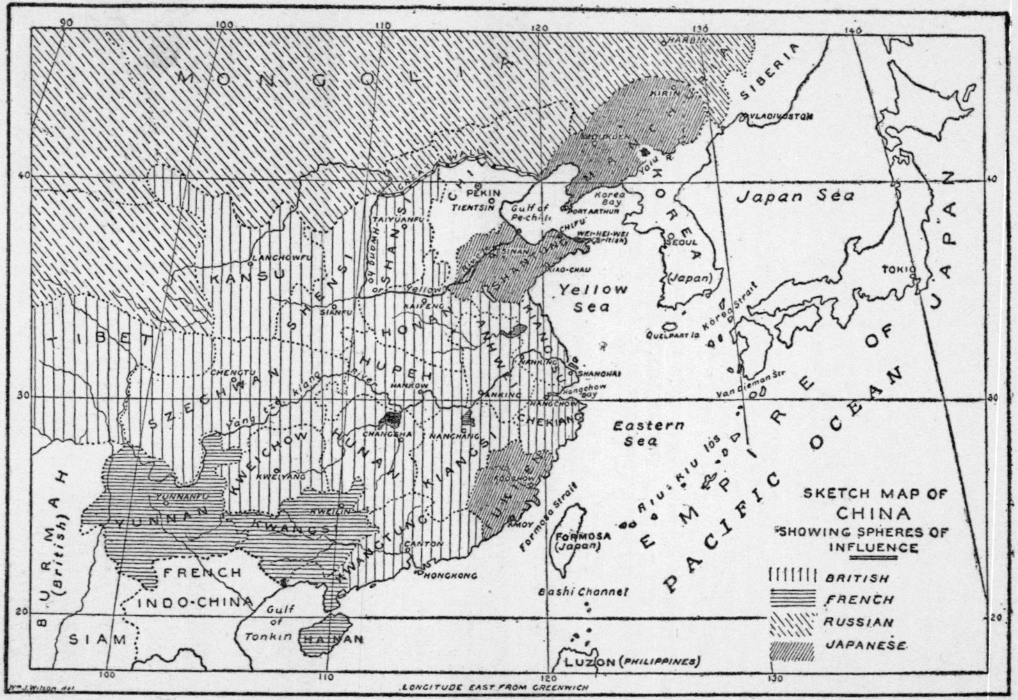
SKETCH MAP OF
CHINA
SHOWING SPHERES OF
INFLUENCE
BRITISH
FRENCH
RUSSIAN
JAPANESE
MONGOLIA
SIBERIA
MANCHURIA
KOREA
(Japan)
JAPAN
EMPIRE OF JAPAN
PACIFIC OCEAN
Japan Sea
Yellow Sea
Eastern Sea
Gulf of Pe-chi-li
Korea Bay
Korea Strait
Van Dieman Str
Formosa Strait
Bashi Channel
Gulf of Tonkin
FORMOSA (Japan)
LUZON (PHILIPPINES)
HAINAN
TIBET
KANSU
SHENSI
SHANSI
CHILI
SHANTUNG
HONAN
KIANGSU
ANHWEI
HUPEH
SZECHWAN
KWEICHOW
HUNAN
KIANGSI
CHEKIANG
FUKIEN
YUNNAN
KWANGSI
KWANGTUNG
FRENCH INDO-CHINA
BURMAH (British)
SIAM
HARBIN
KIRIN
MOUKDEN
VLADIVOSTOK
Yalu R.
PEKIN
TIENTSIN
PORT ARTHUR
CHIFU
WEI-HEI-WEI (British)
SEOUL
TOKIO
QUELPART Id
KIAO-CHAU
TSINAN
TAIYUANFU
LANCHOWFU
SIANFU
KAIFENG
Hwang ho or Yellow
NANKING
SHANGHAI
Hangchow Bay
HANGCHOW
ANKING
HANKOW
CHENGTU
Yang tze kiang River
CHANGSHA
NANCHANG
KWEIYANG
YUNNANFU
KWEILIN
FOOCHOW
AMOY
CANTON
HONGKONG
GREAT WALL
Riu-Kiu Is
90
100
110
120
130
140
40
30
20
LONGITUDE EAST FROM GREENWICH
Wm J. Wilson del.

PEKING DUST

I

POOR OLD CHINA

WHEN I came away last August, you said you wanted me to tell you about our travels, particularly about China. Like most Americans, you have a lurking sentimental feeling about China, a latent sympathy and interest based on colossal ignorance. Very well, I will write you as fully as I can. Two months ago my ignorance was fully as overwhelming as yours, but it is being rapidly dispelled. So I 'll try to do the same for you, as you said I might. Rash of you, I call it.

I 'll take it that you have just about heard that China is on the map, and occupies a big portion of it. You know that she has a ruler of some kind in place of the old empress dowager who died a few years ago. Come to think of it, the ruler is a president, and China is a republic. Vaguely you may remember that she became a republic about five years ago, after a revolution. Also, in the same vague way, you may have heard that the country is old and rich and peaceful, with about four hundred million inhabitants; and beyond that you do not go. Sufficient. I 'll go no further, either.

After six weeks in Japan, we set out for Peking, going by way of Korea. On the boat from Kobe to Shimonoseki, passing through the famous Inland Sea of Japan,—which, by the way, reminds one of the eastern shore of Maryland,—we met a young Englishman returning to Shanghai. We three, being the only first-class passengers on the boat, naturally fell into conversation. He said he had been in the East for ten years, engaged in business in Shanghai, so we at once dashed into the subject of Oriental politics. Being quite ignorant of Eastern affairs, but having heard vaguely of certain phases of them, we asked if he could tell us the meaning of "sphere of influence." The Orient seems full of spheres of influence, particularly China.

"How do the European nations acquire these 'spheres of influence' in China?" I asked. "Do they ask the Chinese Government to give them to them?—to set apart certain territory, certain provinces, and give them commercial and trading rights to these areas?"

"Ask the Chinese Government?" repeated the young man, scornfully. "Ask the Chinese? I should say not! The European powers just arrange it among themselves, each decides what provinces it wants, agrees not to trespass upon the spheres of influence of one another, and then they just notify China."

"Just notify China?" I exclaimed. "You mean they don't consult China at all and find out whether she 's willing or not? You mean they just decide the matter among themselves, partition out the country as they like, select such territory as they happen to fancy, and then just notify China?"

"That 's the idea," he returned; "virtually

that 's all there is to it. Choose what they want and then just notify China."

"Dear me!" said I.

I 'm glad we met that young man. I like things put simply, in words of one syllable, within range of the understanding. Moreover, incredible as it seems, what he told us is true. Oh, of course, as I 've found out since, there are treaties and things to be signed after China has been notified. She is then compelled to ratify these treaties or agreements; it looks better. Forced to sign them at the pistol's point, as it were. However, this ratification of treaties is more for the benefit of the European powers than for China. Having staked out their claims, they officially record them; that 's all. And you know what used to happen in our country during the good old days of the "forty-niners" if some one jumped another's claim.

To show to what extent poor old China is under the "influence" of the great European powers, I shall have to give you a few statistics; otherwise you won't believe me. The total area of the Chinese Republic is about 4,300,000 square miles. The spheres of influence of some of the important nations are as follows:

		Square miles
England:	Tibet	533,000
	Szechuen	218,000
	Kwan'tung	86,000
	Provinces of Yangtse Valley	362,000
	Total	1,199,000 or 27.8%
Russia:	Outer Mongolia	1,000,000
	Che-Kiang	548,000
	Three-quarters of Manchuria	273,000
	Total	1,821,000 or 42.3%
France:	Yunnan	146,700 or 3.4%
Germany:	Shan-tung	55,000 or 1.3%
Japan:	South Manchuria	90,000
	Eastern Inner Mongolia	50,000
	Fu-kien	46,000
	Total	186,000 or 4.3%
Total area under foreign influence		79%

Don't forget these figures; turn back to them from time to time to refresh your memory. But remember one thing: it is not customary to speak of anything but of Japanese aggression. Whenever Japan acquires another square mile of territory, forestalling some one else, the fact is heralded round the world, and the predatory tendencies of Japan are denounced as a menace to the world. But publicity is not given to the predatory tendencies of other powers. They are all in agreement with one another, and nothing is said; a conspiracy of silence surrounds their actions, and the facts are smothered, not a hint of them getting abroad. The Western nations are in accord, and the Orient—China—belongs to them. But with Japan it is different. So in future, when you hear that Japan has her eye on China, is attempting to gobble up China, remember that, compared with Europe's total, Japan's holdings are very small indeed. The loudest outcries against Japanese encroachments come from those nations that possess the widest spheres of influence. The nation that claims forty-two per cent. of China, and the nation that claims twenty-seven per cent. of China are loudest in their denunciations of the nation that possesses (plus the former German holdings) less than six.

Our first actual contact with a sphere of influence at work came about in this wise: After we had spent two or three weeks in Korea, we took the train from Seoul to Peking, a two-days' journey. In these exciting days it is hard to do without newspapers, and at Mukden, where we had a five-hours' wait, we came across a funny little sheet called "The Manchuria Daily News." It was a nice little paper; that is, if you are sufficiently cosmopolitan to be emancipated from American standards. It was ten by fifteen inches in size,—comfortable to hold, at any rate,—with three pages of news and advertisements, and one blank page for which nothing was forthcoming. Tucked in among advertisements of mineral waters, European groceries, foreign banking-houses, and railway announcements was an item. But for our young man on the boat, I should n't have known what it meant. We read:

ALLIES PROTEST TO CHINA

Great Britain, France and Russia have lodged their respective protests with China on the ground that the Sino-American railway loan agreement recently concluded, infringes upon their acquired rights. The Russian contention is that the construction of the railway from Fengchen to Ninghsia conflicts with the 1899 Russo-Chinese Secret Treaty. The British point out that the Hangchow-Wenchow railway under scheme is a violation of the Anglo-Chinese Treaty re Hunan and Kwanghsi, and that the proposed railway constitutes a trespass on the British preferential right to build railways. The French Government, on behalf of Belgium, argues that the Lanchow-Ninghsia line encroaches upon the Sino-Belgian Treaty re the Haichow-Lanchow Railway, and that the railway connecting Hangchow with Nanning intrudes upon the French sphere of influence.

There you have it! China needing a railway, an American firm willing to build a railway, and Russia, England, France, and even poor little Belgium blocking the scheme. All of them busy with a tremendous war on their hands, draining all their resources of both time and money, yet able to keep a sharp eye on China to see that she does n't get any improvements that are not of their making. And after the war is over, how many years will it be before they are sufficiently recovered financially to undertake such an expenditure? China must just wait, I suppose.

On each side of the rocking railway carriage stretched vast arid plains, sprinkled with innumerable villages consisting of mud houses. The fields were cut across in every direction by dirt roads, unpaved, full of deep ruts and holes. At times these roads were sunk far below the level of the fields, worn deep into the earth by the traffic of centuries; so deep in places that the tops of the blue-hooded carts were also below the level of the fields. Yet these roads afford the only means of communication with the immense interior provinces of China—these sunken roads and the rivers.

Just then we passed a procession of camels, and for a moment I forgot all about the article in "The Manchuria Daily News." Who would n't, seeing camels on the landscape! A whole long caravan of them, several hundred, all heavily laden, and moving in slow, majestic dignity at the rate of two miles an hour! Coming in from some unknown region of the great Mongolian plains, the method of transportation employed for thousands of years! Yes, undoubtedly, China needs railways; but she can't have any more at present, for she has no money to construct them herself, and the great nations who claim seventy-nine per cent. of her soil have n't time at present to build them for her. And they object to letting America do it. A sphere of influence is a dog in the manger.

II

PEKING

HERE we are in Peking at last, the beautiful, barbaric capital of China, the great, gorgeous capital of Asia. For Peking is the capital of Asia, of the whole Orient, the center of the stormy politics of the Far East. We are established at the Grand Hôtel des Wagons-Lits, called locally the "Bed-Wagon Hotel," or, as the marines say, the "Wagon Slits." It is the most interesting hotel in the world, too, where the nations of the world meet, rub elbows, consult together, and plan to "do" one another and China, too. It is entertaining to sit in the dark, shabby lounge and watch the passers-by, or to dine in the big, shabby, gilded dining-room, and see the various types gathered there, talking together over big events, or over little events that have big consequences. Peking is not a commercial city, not a business center; it is not filled with drummers or traveling-men or small fry of that kind, such as you find in Shanghai and lesser places. It is the diplomatic and political center of the Orient, and here are the people who are at the top of things, no matter how shady the things. At least it is the top man in the concern who is here to promote its interests.

Here are the big concession-hunters of all nationalities, with headquarters in the hotel, ready to sit tight for a period of weeks or months or as long as it may take to wheedle or bribe or threaten the Chinese Government into granting them what they wish—a railroad, a bank, a mine, a treaty port. Over in a corner of the lounge sits a so-called princess, a Chinese lady, very modern, very chic, very European as to clothes, who was formerly one of the ladies-in-waiting to the old empress dowager. And, by the way, it took a woman to hold China together. Next to her sits a young Chinese gentleman, said to be the grandson of one of the old prime ministers, a slim, dapper youth, spectacled and intelligent. I may say that the lady is almost completely surrounded by the young man, but no one gives them more than a passing glance. We do, because we are new-comers, but the others are used to it. The British adviser to the Chinese Government passes, a tall, distinguished, gray-haired man, talking with a burly Englishman, hunter of big game, but now, according to rumor, a member of the secret service. Concession-hunters and business men sit about in groups, representatives of great commercial and banking firms from all over the world. A minister from some legation drops in; there are curio-buyers from Europe, with a sprinkling of tourists, and a tired-looking, sallow group of anemic men and women who have just come up from Manila on an army transport.

The approach to Peking is tremendously impressive. Lying in an arid plain, the great, gray walls, with their magnificent towers, rise dignified and majestic. Over the tops of the walls nothing is to be seen. There are no skyscrapers within; no house is higher than the surrounding, defending ramparts. Peking is divided into several areas, each called a city, each city surrounded by its own walls. There is the great, populous Chinese City, where only the Chinese dwell. The Tartar, or Manchu, City has several subdivisions. It contains the legation quarter, and all the foreign legations are clustered together in a small, compact area, surrounded by a small wall for defensive purposes. Beyond the legation quarter, on all sides, extends the Tartar City itself. Foreigners also live in this part of Peking, and, as far as I can see, always hold themselves in readiness to dash to the protection of their legation if anything goes wrong. They tell one that it is quite safe, that nothing can go wrong, that the Boxer troubles can never be repeated; but all the same, they always appear to have a bag packed and a ladder leaning against the compound walls in case of emergency. Which gives life in Peking a delightful flavor of suspense and excitement.

Also within the Tartar City lies the Imperial

City, inclosed by towering red walls, and within that lies the Forbidden City, residence of the rulers of China, containing the palaces, and the dwelling-places of the mandarins. Now, except for certain parts of the Forbidden City, such as the palace of the President, Li Yuan Hung, the city is no longer forbidden. It is open to the public, and the public may come and go at will; coolies, hucksters, beggars, foreigners—all may move freely within the sacred precincts where formerly none but the high and mighty might venture.

The streets are marvelous. Those in the legation quarter are well paved, European, and stupid; but those in the Chinese and Tartar cities are full of excitement. A few are wide, but the majority are narrow, winding alleys, and all alike are packed and crowded with people and animals and vehicles of all kinds. Walking is a matter of shoving oneself through the throng, dodging under camels' noses, avoiding wheelbarrows, bumping against donkeys, standing aside to let officials' carriages go by,—antiquated European carriages, very shabby but surrounded by outriders, mounted on shaggy Mongolian ponies, who gallop ahead and clear the way. The horses can't be guided from behind; the coachman sits on the box and holds the reins and looks impressive, but the real work is done by the *mafu* or groom. When it comes to turning a corner, passing a camel-train, or other obstacle, the *mafu* is obliged to leap down from his seat, seize the bridle, and lead the horses round whatever obstruction there may be. At other times, when not leading the horses, the *mafu* sits on the box and shouts to clear the way. I tell you, progress in a carriage is a noisy affair,—what with the rattling of the old vehicle, the clanking of the brass-mounted harness, the yells and screams of the groom, and the yells and shouts of the crowds refusing to give way. It 's barbaric, but has a certain style and swing.

Don't think there is any speed to a carriage. Oh, no. Despite the noise and rattle and apparent progress, the progress itself is very slow. At the rate of two miles an hour, possibly. We went out for a drive in the minister's carriage the other day, a comfortable victoria, drawn by a pair of very fat, very sorrel horses, and we skimmed along, as I say, at the rate of two miles an hour when the going was good. All we passed were the pedestrians,—a few of them,—and we usually found ourselves tailing along behind a camel-train or waiting for a wheelbarrow to get out of the way. In the side streets, or *hutungs,* we shouted ourselves along at a snail's pace, cleaving the dense throngs of inattentive citizens, whose right to the middle of the road was as great as ours, and who did n't purpose to be disturbed. Once on turning a corner, the groom pulled the bridle off one of the horses. Off it slipped into his hand, and the horse tossed his head and ran. The *mafu* yelled, the coachman yelled, every one else yelled, and for a few moments there was intense excitement. Later on, that same afternoon, we went out to tea somewhere, this time going by rickshaw. In comparison to the speed of a carriage, the pace of a rickshaw-runner is prodigious. We were positively dizzy.

There is a great difference between the speed of the rickshaw-runners in Tokyo and in Peking. In Japan they go rather slowly, and refuse to overexert themselves, and quite right, too; but here they go at top speed. There are such enormous numbers of them, and competition is so keen, that the swift young runners make capital of their strength. It is pathetic to see broken-down old coolies, panting and blowing, making painful efforts to compete with the younger men. I am not yet used to being taken about by man-power. It seems wrong somehow, demoralizing, for one human being to place himself in that humiliating relation to another, to become a draft animal, to be forced to lower himself to the level of an ox or an ass. It must have an insidious, demoralizing effect, too, upon the persons who ride in these little vehicles. I am not yet used to seeing able-bodied young foreigners, especially men, being pulled about by thin, tired, exhausted coolies. I feel ashamed every time I enter a rickshaw and contrast my well-being with that of the ragged boy between the shafts.

Coolies

Camel caravan, Peking

I suppose I shall get over this feeling, think no more about it than any one else does, but at present it is new to me. Every time we leave the hotel, twenty boys dash forward, all clamoring for us; and if we decide to walk, twenty disappointed, half-starved boys wheel their little buggies back to the curb again and wait. Well, what can one do? They are so desperately poor! One way or the other, it seems all wrong.

We got caught in a block in the Chinese City the other day. At the intersection of two cross streets, narrow little *hutungs* about eight feet wide, four streams of traffic collided, and got hopelessly entangled in a yelling, unyielding snarl. From one direction came a camel-train from Mongolia; from another, three or four blue-hooded, long-axled, Peking carts. Along a third street came a group of water-carriers and wheelbarrows, and from the fourth half a dozen rickshaws. All met, and in a moment became thoroughly mixed up. There being no traffic regulation of any kind, no right of way of any sort, there was no idea in the mind of any one but that of his unalterable right to go ahead. It was pandemonium in a minute, with yells and curses, pushing and blows, men whacking one another and the beasts indiscriminately. Over the tops of the blue-hooded carts the tall camels raised their scornful heads, and surveyed the commotion with aloof disdain. In all the world there is nothing so arrogant and haughty as a camel, and they regarded from their supercilious height the petty quarreling of man. In fifteen minutes, however, the snarl cleared itself up, and it was the camels who first managed to slither by, after which each vehicle unwound itself from the mess and passed on.

You know, the lobby of this hotel seems a little like that block of traffic. There is such a heterogeneous massing of nationalities and of people within these shabby walls—officials, soldiers, concession-hunters, tourists, attachés, journalists, explorers. All those camels, coolies, rickshaw-boys, and water-carriers each felt that he had the right of way; and so all these people think that they have the right of way in China. There must be a hundred different opinions about China in these corridors of the hotel. I 'll see what I can discover.

III

CIVILIZATION

THE longer we stay here, the more we are impressed with the fact that in China there is no sympathy for the Allies. The atmosphere is not at all pro-German, however. There is no special feeling for the Central powers any more than there is for the Entente Allies. It can best be described as neutrality, or, rather, complete indifference as to which group wins. Coming as we have direct from France,—two years of France in war-time,—it is very curious to find ourselves plunged into this atmosphere of total indifference to the outcome and objects of the war. We have gathered these impressions from many talks with the Chinese and from a diligent perusal of Chinese papers,—papers printed in English, but owned and edited by the Chinese, and which may therefore be said to reflect their sentiments. Also we have talked with many foreigners who have lived in China for a long time, who have many Chinese friends and acquaintances, and understand the Chinese point of view, and these also tell us that China has no sympathy with the Allies or with any other powers.

The explanation is not hard to find. Despite what foreigners may think of them, the Chinese are by no means fools. They possess the wisdom of the ages,—of their own peculiar kind. They have had a long experience with foreigners, saddening and enriching, and cynicism is the outgrowth of such experience. China has suffered at the hands of the great powers, has suffered at the hands of England, Russia, France, and Germany alike. She is virtually in the position of a vassal state, not to any one of these nations but to all of them, and they have pillaged and despoiled her for a century and a half. To one of them she owes the curse of opium, which was forced upon her for commercial reasons—a curse which she is about ready to throw off. She is weak and corrupt, but it is to the advantage of her foreign masters to keep her in a state of weakness and corruption. At the present moment she is paying huge indemnities to various European powers as compensation for the losses they sustained during the Boxer uprising in 1900, the Boxer trouble being an attempt on the part of China to rid herself of the foreign invader. To one of these countries, Russia, she is paying an indemnity part of which consists of the expenses of thousands of troops which had no existence except on paper. It is hardly possible for the Chinese to believe, in the light of their own experience, that the various European nations at death-grips in this war are actuated by the noble sentiments they profess to be fighting for. The assurances from Europe, cabled daily to the Chinese press, that the Allies are fighting for liberty, for justice, for civilization, for the protection of small nations, mean nothing to the Chinese. Such professions leave them cold. To the Oriental mind this gigantic struggle is between a nation who is mistress of the world (and the world's markets) and a nation who wishes to become mistress of the world (and the world's markets). With seventy-nine per cent. of her territory under foreign control, China can hardly believe in the disinterested motives of the fighting nations.

The other day I saw a little incident on the street that puts the case in a nutshell. Two big Mongolian dogs were locked together in a fight to the death. Each had the other in a death-grip, and they rolled over and over in the dust, surrounded by a great crowd of people who stood by indifferently and watched them fight it out. This is the attitude of China toward the European War, the attitude of the calm, indifferent spectator.

The structure of civilization that Europe has erected for itself is imposing and beautiful. We in America are confronted with the façade of this great building, and beheld from our side of the Atlantic it looks magnificent and superb. Even when we enter it in Europe, and behold its many ramifications, we still have cause to admire. But there is a back side to this structure of civilization; there are outbuildings, slums, and alleys not visible from the front. These back on the Orient, and the rear view of the structure of European civilization, seen from the Orient, is not imposing at all. The sweepings and refuse of Western civilization and Western morality are dumped out upon the Orient, where they do not show.

IV

RACE ANTAGONISMS

IT is a crisp, cold morning, but nothing to what it will be, they tell us, when the autumn is over, and the bitter winter settles down upon North China. After all, come to think of it, we are abutting on two extremely Northern provinces, Manchuria and Mongolia, and these adjoin Siberia, which all the world knows is cold. So this sharp October day, with its brilliant blue sky and hard, glittering sunshine, is only a foretaste of the weather that will come later.

To-day we went into the Chinese City and visited a native department store. At the best speed of our rickshaw-boys we passed out of the Chi'en Men, the principal gate, and once beyond the towering, embattled wall that separates the Chinese from the Tartar City, we lost ourselves in the maze of narrow, winding streets that open on all sides from the main road leading from the Chi'en Men, which, by the way, has been in the possession of the American troops since the Boxer uprising. In the narrow *hutungs* our progress was slow; we literally shoved our way through crowds of rickshaws and thousands of pedestrians, and as there are no sidewalks, we were alternately scraping the walls and shop fronts on one hand, or locking wheels with Peking carts on the other, and feeling the warm breath of a camel or donkey down our necks whenever the traffic brought us to a halt. Finally our boys stopped before a large building about three stories high, emblazoned with gold dragons, and with gorgeous red and yellow banners and flags all over the front of it. It stood some distance back from the street, and the wide courtyard in front was filled and crowded with the carts and carriages of the high-class women who had gone inside to shop.

I have already told you that Chinese horses can't be driven; they must be led along with great show and shouting. Well, when they stop they can't even be trusted to stay in harness; they must be unharnessed and removed to a place of safety. Therefore the courtyard of this department store presented a unique appearance, filled with twenty or thirty Peking carts, empty, tilted back on their haunches, with shafts gaping toward heaven. Also, the horses had been removed from innumerable little coupés of ancient date, with the superstructure all of glass, so that the occupant within is completely visible from all sides, like a fish in an aquarium. Horses and mules, in gorgeous, glittering harness, were carefully stood apart, or were being led up and down in the crowded courtyard to cool off. Though why cool off, after a dash through the streets at two miles an hour or less, I could n't see. However, here they all were,—great, high white horses, shaggy Mongolian ponies, and magnificent mules, the latter by far the most superb animals I 've ever seen. I am not much at heights, but the mules were enormously tall, enormously heavy, very beautiful beasts, white, red, yellow, and black, and sleek with unlimited polishing and grooming. They were clad—that 's the only word—in heavy, barbaric harness, mounted with huge brass buckles, and in some cases the leather was studded with jade, carnelian, and other semi-precious stones.

Style? There 's nothing on Fifth Avenue to touch it. Do you think a ten-thousand-dollar automobile is handsome? It 's nothing to a Peking cart, with its huge, sleek mule and glittering harness. I tell you, the Chinese have the style of the world; the rest of us are but imitators. In comparison, our motors are merest upstarts. But you must picture a Peking cart, of beautifully polished wood, natural color, and a heavy wooden body covered with a big blue hood. The owner rides inside, on cushions, and on each shaft sits a servant, one to hold the reins, the other to yell and jump off and run forward to press his weight on the shaft to lessen the jar to the occupant whenever a bad bit of road presents itself. They say that this old custom, due to the discomfort and jolting of the springless carts, is the reason why the horses are not

Peking cart

Fruit stall in the bazaar

trained to round corners or go over bad bits of road alone. From time immemorial it has been the duty of the groom to run forward and throw his weight on the shafts to lessen the jolts; therefore he is the real, the important driver. In front of the blue-linen hood hangs a curtain, and the two side windows are also carefully curtained, with screens which permit the occupant to see out but not to be seen from without. Thus do high-class mandarins protect themselves, save themselves from having to descend whenever they meet a mandarin of equal or higher rank and prostrate themselves in the dust before him. Also, the longer the axle, the further it projects beyond the hub of the wheel, the higher the rank of the owner; it denotes his right to occupy the road. The rims of the wheels are spiked: big nails project all round, indicating the mandarin's right to tear up the road. It 's all splendid and barbaric; no mawkish sentiment about it.

So we entered the department store through rows and rows, very neat and orderly, of upturned carts and antiquated coupés, and mules and horses and a courtyard full of liveried servants. Inside, it still looked barbaric, with its magnificent display of rich silks and furs. Great skins of tiger, panther, leopard, wildcat, sable, were hanging in profusion on all sides, interspersed with costly embroideries, wonderful brocades, and all the magnificence and color of the gorgeous East. It was the idea of Kwong, our pet rickshaw-boy, to bring us here and we soon found that foreigners were not expected and not wanted. No one of the suave shop attendants could speak English, nor did they make the slightest attempt to wait on us. We wandered round, rather desolate, followed by looks of curiosity and disdain on the part of the clerks, and the wholly undisguised amusement and contempt of the high-class Chinese and Manchu women, who, with their liveried servants, were making the rounds of the various floors. In the store it was noisy and cheerful, the atmosphere cold and close except in the neighborhood of a few big red-hot stoves, which gave forth a local heat. Chinese women, not high-class, attired in satin trousers, sat about at small tables drinking tea and smoking cigarettes, tea and cigarettes being furnished free at innumerable little tables on every floor. As we passed, they giggled and nudged one another. Can't you imagine a Chinese lady in satin trousers passing through a great American department store and being remarked upon? To them we were equally queer, and they made no attempt to disguise the fact. There was none of that servile deference one finds among the hotel servants and the rickshaw-boys, or of the extreme politeness of the upper-class Chinese whom we had met at the legations and elsewhere. To these people we were nothing but foreigners, and down at heart foreigners excite nothing but amusement or hostility. That conservative, gossiping throng of Orientals had a good, firm opinion of us, and it was n't complimentary. We were interlopers and intruders, and had no business in that *pukkah* Chinese shop. We were glad to get out and to make our purchases in some kindlier atmosphere.

How can I reconcile this impression with previous ones, of the docility and servility we had previously encountered? Docility and subserviency are necessary in dealing with the conquering foreigner, but in such places and on such occasions when those qualities are not required, we get an impression of the real feelings of the Chinese. I believe they feel toward us very much as we should feel toward them, or toward any other nation that claimed us as a vassal state. For one country to be under the "influence" of another, for any nation to assert a "benevolent protectorate" over another, is to engender the hostility of the state so patronized. Very well, it stands to reason. Foreigners have been patting China on the head for a long time, and repeated pats don't always produce a callous; sometimes they produce profound irritation.

This country is so enormous, so chaotic, one is so aware of the strength underlying its calm, submissive exterior, that one feels that some day this latent strength will break through and disclose itself. In trying to describe all these feelings at random, day by day as they come, I am not trying to sort them out and classify them and present them in an orderly manner. You must see them with me, and feel them with me from day to day, and do your own thinking later. That English boy on the boat coming over to China told us this. We asked him if he had enjoyed his vacation in Japan.

"Not much, he replied. "I don't care for the Japanese; they don't compare with the Chinese."

"What 's the difference?" I asked.

He pondered a moment.

"I 'll sum it up for you like this," he answered. "In Japan they treat you as an equal; in China they treat you as a superior."

That 's it, I believe. Race antagonism all the way through. China is a conquered country. She does n't dare show resentment or insist upon equality. Whatever her private opinion may be, she is helpless, and she must treat her conquerors with deference as superiors. But Japan has never been conquered by the foreigner. She is the only nation among all the nations of the Orient that has never been trodden underfoot by the European. She has never been subjugated and never been drugged. And, curious coincidence, she has reached a level with the foremost powers of the world, and holds the rank of a first-class nation. All this without having had the blessings of European civilization conferred upon her by a conqueror! She has snatched here and there, has imitated, even excelled, certain qualities and propensities of the white man, but has never been blighted by having Western civilization forced upon her. That 's the rub. Japan is a striking example to the rest of Asia; her success is a striking commentary on the value of independence. She has attained eminence without the assistance of the great powers. And of the value of this assistance, conferred by the great powers upon the other nations of Asia—enough said.

V

SPHERES OF INFLUENCE

WE are beginning to know a lot of people in Peking, for we were launched upon Peking society the other night when we dined at the American legation. It was the first dinner party we have been to in several years, as we have been living quietly in Paris since the beginning of the war, and there are no such things as dinners or parties in Paris in these distressful days. However, knowing that we were coming to the Orient, and having shrewd ideas that possibly we might be invited out, and therefore would need a proper dress, E—— and I each had one made, a good one. Strange and unusual sensation to get into them; neither of us could tell the back from the front! They looked alike from both aspects, and felt equally uncomfortable either way. We tried them on both ways and got no light from the experience, and then laid them on the bed and looked at them ruminatively, all the while the clock moving toward eight and no decision reached.

Finally, we concluded that if there was as little difference between back and front as that, it could n't matter much. Which shows you how little we have been wearing evening clothes in the last two years, and how unaccustomed to them we are. So, as I say, we dined at the legation the other night, with our dresses on hind-side before, for all we knew, and neither of us was troubled at all. Had a delightful time, too, and met many interesting people. The dinner was in honor of the general in charge of our army in the Philippines, and we also met Admiral von Hinze, the German minister. The Dutch minister and his wife were there, too. As America is neutral, it is necessary to entertain the various diplomats as usual, but naturally they can't all dine at the legation on the same evening. Sheep and goats, as it were, one dinner to the Allied representatives, the next to the representatives of the Central powers. Much nice sorting is required, and they tell us that in consequence of the war Peking society is rift in twain. This is all very well when it happens in a big community, but when it happens in such a limited little society as Peking, all walled in together within the narrow inclosure of the legation quarter,—walled in literally, also, in the fullest sense, with soldiers from the guards of the various legations patrolling the walls and mounting guard day and night,—such a situation results in great tension and embarrassment all round. There was not one word of war talk during the dinner; it was tacitly avoided, by common consent.

Well, as I said, after that dinner the other night, people began to be very nice to us and to invite us out. The one safe subject for discussion is Chinese politics, in which every one is interested and of which every one knows a lot. At least, I don't know that they really know, but they say they do, and speak as if they do, and become emphatic if you doubt them, and altogether they dispense a wonderful lot of news, whatever its value. Rumors! There was never in the world such a place for rumors as Peking. We thought Paris was the hotbed of rumors during the last two years of the war—Paris with its censored press, suppressed speech, and general military rule, so that all one lives on are the rumors that never get into the papers; but Peking is stupendous. Here the rumors simply fly, and the corridors of the old Wagons-Lits Hotel seems to be the pivotal spot of the whirlwind. Sooner or later every one in Peking seems to drop into the hotel on some pretext or other, as if it were a club, and the lounge is so thick with news and rumor and gossip that you can lean up against them and not fall down. All absolutely true, authentic, unquestionable, and to-morrow all flatly contradicted by another set equally veracious, startling, and imposing. Never mind. Who are we, to question the truth of them? All we can do is to drink them in day by day, modify and change our opinions on the morrow, and enjoy ourselves with such thrills as one gets nowhere else in the civilized world.

On top of it all we have the newspapers. There are three or four in English, one in French, and the rest in the vernacular. The most interesting is "The Peking Gazette," since it represents the pure Chinese point of view. Printed in English, it is owned and edited by the Chinese, and gives their side of the story. The editor is a delightful man, Chinese, an Oxford graduate, fiery, intense, alert, ever on the defensive for China's rights and speaking in no uncertain tones on that subject, leaving one in no doubt as to his attitude on a decision concerning China's welfare when opposed to the welfare of a European nation that wishes to "do" China. "The Daily News" is the organ of the Allied powers, and presents things from the point of view of the Western nations; consequently there is perpetual warfare between the "Gazette" and the "News," the perpetual clash between Chinese and foreign interests. Only on one subject do they agree—their hatred of Japan. For the Chinese do not like Japan any more than they like any other would-be conqueror. And the Europeans do not like Japan, who is their great commercial rival, a rival that can market her products without going half-way round the world. Consequently the "News" attacks Japan, while the "Gazette" attacks impartially all invaders who seek the subjection of China. It is amusing. When the "Gazette" attacks Japan, a chorus of praise from the European organs. When it attacks predatory tendencies manifested by European nations, a chorus of denunciation from the European organs. But the editor fights ahead, regardless of praise or blame, with a single purpose in view, the preservation of China's sovereignty.

A few days ago this article appeared in the "Gazette," an amplification of the little paragraph in that diminutive newspaper "The Manchuria Daily News" of which I wrote you. Said the "Gazette," under a bold head-line in large type:

CHINA IN FETTERS

Foreign writers are wont to complain that nothing in the sense of real work is being done in this country. This, of course, is a misleading statement, although much that ought to be done is left undone. And one of the principal reasons for this state of things is revealed in what begins to look like the development of a scandalous opposition to American enterprise in China. Owing to the war putting a stop to the financing of public undertakings in China by European capitalists and contractors, a powerful American organization has turned its attention to this country and in an entirely business sense has secured contracts for the construction of certain railroads in China. The transaction involves the expenditure of $200,000,000 of American money, a considerable portion of which will be spent for labor and other things. It is admitted that there is absolutely nothing like "politics" in the deal. The same remark applies with greater force to the American loan for the conservency of a portion of the Grand Canal. And yet we have Japan, Russia, France, Great Britain, and even *Belgium*—a country that ought at least to know what not to do to a state struggling to preserve its elementary rights of existence—trying to interfere with the construction of necessary public works in this country, simply because America can do what these other people cannot now do.

"China in Fetters"—a significant term for a Chinese newspaper to use. It would seem as if these spheres of influence[1] had become linked together into a chain for throttling purposes. I tried to tell you the other day about them, but please listen to a little further explanation. In the lobby of the hotel I found a journalist who knows things, who had been in China many years.

"Explain to me," I asked him, "all over, from the very beginning, what these things mean."

"The country which claims such a sphere," he began patiently, "claims for itself the right to develop that territory."

"Suppose," I interrupted, "the Chinese themselves should wish to develop this territory,—to open up a gold-mine, to build a railway,—would they be allowed to do so?"

"Certainly, if they have the money."

"But if they have n't the money, if they must borrow?"

[1] America has neither a concession nor a sphere of influence in all China.

"Then they must borrow from the power which claims the territory."

"But if for some reason that power can't lend it to them,—can't spare it, as is the case with all Europe at present,—or if for some other reason does not wish to lend it, what then?"

He shrugged his shoulders.

"Fineesh! China can't borrow money from one power to 'start something' in the sphere of influence claimed by another."

Apropos of all this there 's a good story at present going the rounds of Peking. The head of a certain great corporation, out here seeking a concession from the Chinese Government, appeared before the Chinese officials one day and made his request. The officials, in their gorgeous robes, were all seated round a large table on which was spread a map of China. It was a wonderful large map, but all colored in different colors, some parts red, some blue, others yellow, and so on. Behind the chairs of the Chinese officials stood the representatives of the various European powers—British, French, Russian, all of them. Our American laid his finger on that part of the map colored red.

"I 'll do the work here," he said to the Chinese.

"Excuse me," interrupted a representative of a foreign government, "you can't go there. That red part of China belongs to Great Britain."

"Very well. I 'll go here," said the American, indicating the blue part of the map.

"Excuse me," said another European gentleman, "you can't do it there. That part of China belongs to Russia."

"Here, then," continued the American, laying his finger on a green spot. "This will do."

Another suave alert diplomatic gentleman stepped forth.

"That," he said regretfully, "is French."

So it went on all over the map. The Chinese officials sat silent, while one European representative after another stepped forward with his objections. Finally, in exasperation, the American turned to the silent Chinese and asked:

"Where the hell is China?"

VI

ON THE SACREDNESS OF FOREIGNERS

YOU know, I can't believe that it is good for us,—Americans, Europeans, foreigners of all sorts,—to feel ourselves so sacred as we feel in China. Whatever we do, we are always right, no matter how wrong we may be. We always have the right of way, the privilege of walking over the Chinese, and to this privilege they must submit. Our sacredness is not due to admiration for or belief in us. Quite the contrary. It is due to a deep sense of fear of the consequences should they attempt to check or curb our activities or inclinations. The relations between a subject people and their conquerors is fundamentally immoral, and demoralizing to both. A few years ago motors made their appearance in Peking; there are not many even to-day. But there are no speed regulations, and they dash through the crowded streets as rapidly as they choose. After a number of accidents the Chinese sought to establish a speed-limit law, but this was positively objected to by one of the foreign ministers, who said that he did not intend to have his liberty interfered with by the Chinese!

Throughout China are the foreign concessions, small holdings of land which belong to the various European nations. In each of the treaty ports these concessions are established, —Russian, English, French, German,—and although they lie in the heart of a Chinese city, they are absolutely the property of the Russians, English, French, or Germans, as the case may be. The Chinese have no authority or control over them, and are unable to regulate them in any way. This brings about a very difficult situation for the Chinese. For example, the opium traffic. On Chinese soil the sale of opium is strictly prohibited; yet it is freely sold in the foreign concessions, and the Chinese are powerless to prevent it. At present they are making a determined and gallant fight against the opium habit, which was forced upon them by Great Britain as the result of two successful opium wars, and legalized by treaties that, to say the least, were extorted from the helpless Chinese. The ratification of these treaties made it all right for Great Britain to import opium as freely as she liked. Well, ten years ago, after a century and a half of opium traffic, poor old China made a stand against this evil and determined to overcome it. She entered into a contract with Great Britain, by the terms of which England agreed to decrease her opium imports year by year, for a period of ten years, in proportion as China decreased, year by year, her poppy cultivation. Both sides have kept the faith, and the end of the bargain will be celebrated by rejoicing (Chinese) on April 1, 1917, when the ten-year contract expires.

It has been a colossal struggle against almost overwhelming odds. For a nation as weak, as unwieldy, as corrupt as China to undertake such a stupendous task seems almost inconceivable. Accurate statistics are not available, but it would seem that one-half of the Chinese were in the grip of this vice. In some provinces about ninety per cent. of the officials were addicted to opium-smoking, and in all provinces a huge percentage of the people were addicts. Anyway, China has made this gigantic effort to get rid of opium, and she has almost succeeded; April 1 of next year will see the end of the whole sordid business. But no assistance has been given her in this enormous task; she has accomplished it alone. During this ten-years' struggle she has had to contend not only against the inclinations of her drug-sodden people but against the fact that her people could procure opium freely in the foreign concessions, over which the Chinese have no control.

The bargain between China and Great Britain, however, has been lived up to. The Chinese began to plant poppies when they were unable to curb or suppress the British imports. As long as the vice was to be fastened upon the country by treaties, they shrewdly decided that at least all the money spent for opium should not go out of the country; therefore they started in on poppy cultivation on their own account. But this native cultivation has been almost entirely suppressed in the last ten years, and the supplies of both native and foreign opium will reach the vanishing-point on April 1, 1917. But it seems pretty hard to realize that the foreign governments have given China no assistance in this struggle. It is too lucrative a trade. The Peking papers are already talking of the great day, only six months distant, when China will have freed herself from this curse. We are determined to be here in Peking to witness the celebration.

But that brings me back to my starting-point, the fact that foreigners are not subject to Chinese laws. In his own concession the foreigner is amenable to the laws of his own country. If on Chinese soil he violates Chinese law, all that the Chinese can do is to hand him to his nearest consul, who may or may not punish him. And this immunity from responsibility, this arrogant privilege of doing as one likes on Chinese soil, with very small chance of being brought to book for it, has a demoralizing influence upon the average foreigner who comes out here. Between ourselves, the class of foreigners who come to China don't amount to much. "Beach-combers" they were called in the good old days—adventurers, gamblers, shady characters of all sorts, and pretty well dwarfed ethically. But no matter what they did, they were usually supported by their various governments, and the result to-day is a well-defined fear of the foreigner, a desire to sidestep him, to stand from under. It seems rather cowardly, this cringing attitude on the part of the Chinese, but it is the result of a century of experience with the ethics of the West. Brave men, unarmed, have been known to throw up their hands in the presence of a bandit.

An amusing thing happened to-day. After tiffin E—— and I went out in our rickshaws, trying to find a shop where we could buy camel's-hair blankets. And, by the way, there are n't any, so we had a fruitless quest. We each have our own rickshaw now, hired by the month at twenty dollars (Mexican) apiece. It seems miserably cheap, yet they tell us that we have paid five dollars more than the usual rate. It was pathetic when we chose our boys the other day—chose two out of a crowd of thirty or more that presented themselves. The disappointment of the others was pitiable. Competition is keen, and it means much to these boys to know they have an assured income rather than haphazard, precarious employment. My boy is called Kwong, and is a wonderful little runner, much faster than E——'s boy.

By this time we are much attached to them, and our days usually end up at the bazaar out on Morrison Street, that marvelous bazaar where everything made in North China is for sale—furs, silks, jade, jewels, sweetmeats, everything. But it is to the sweet-stalls that we always go, where wonderful Chinese candies and sugared fruits are for sale. We first change a dollar into pennies, and then all four of us eat our way from stall to stall—sesame candy, sugared walnuts, sugary plums on straws. It 's wonderful. Germs? Maybe, but we don't care. I am sick of germs, of the emphasis that every one at home places on them. It 's restful to get into a country where there are n't any, or at least people don't know about them. The trouble with America is that every one is so busy thinking of clean streets, clean garbage-cans, the possibilities of disease contained in impure food, that much of the beauty and comfort of life is lost. Life is not all in length.

Well, as I say, with our visit to the bazaar reserved for the end of the afternoon, we went into the Chinese City in search of camel's-hair blankets. Soon we turned aside from the big high-street, and dived into one of the narrow, winding, unpaved lanes of the native city, which only the rickshaw-boys can negotiate. Presently, in this maze of narrow streets, we met the usual block; a dozen rickshaws from opposite directions encountered one another, and each claimed the right of way. When an alley is six feet wide, there is neither right nor way, and voluble conversation ensued, mounting rapidly into screams and curses. Coolies and passengers alike took part in the discussion, and as we were the only foreigners, we felt handicapped by our lack of language. The storm of yells mounted higher and higher, when suddenly the crowd gave way a little, and E——'s boy managed to slide through, while Kwong, pulling me, slipped close behind.

Indignity! It seems the passage had been cleared for a young Chinese gentleman, clad in gorgeous brocade, an official, perhaps, since he had all the marks of wealth and position. As we ran past, into the space opened for him, the young official leaned forward and shouted some insult into Kwong's ear, and Kwong made some furious retort. Instantly the young official jumped from his rickshaw, dashed up to Kwong, and struck him between the eyes. Poor little Kwong staggered, and dropped the shafts, and I leaped out and caught the wrists of the young gentleman just as he was aiming another blow at my unhappy boy. What happened? While I held firmly pinioned the hands of the young gentleman,

Kwong recovered, and proceeded to deal the official a series of stunning blows! He would have fallen except for my hold on his wrists.

"Kwong, stop it! Behave yourself!" I shouted, and released the official in order to seize Kwong. Whereupon the young gentleman pounded Kwong anew. I was unable to hold the hands of both; could seize only one at a time, and my part soon resolved itself into pinioning one belligerent while the other struck him! A silly rôle, I must say. Impartially holding up first one, then the other, for punishment! At a modest estimate, I should say that one half the population of Peking swarmed out of adjacent lanes and burrows to see the excitement, and amidst the pandemonium of yells I heard some one shouting in English: "Police house! Police house!" The finish came when E——'s boy came to the rescue with a hearty kick to the young man, after which the fighters broke away, and every one took to their rickshaws and made off with all speed.

It was too much. To go out on a peaceful

shopping expedition, and become involved in a free-for-all fight! Some one of us lost face by that episode, whether the official, Kwong, or myself, I 'm not sure. There was n't much prestige to the whole thing. Just one fact stands out clearly amidst that maze of swift events. At the end of the street, about fifty feet beyond that wild mob, stood a Chinese policeman. One hasty look he gave to the affair, and seeing that some foreign ladies were involved, he decided to keep out of it. He kept his back turned the entire time, with his hands tight in the pockets of his padded trousers.

VII

DONKEYS GENERALLY

IT 'S all delightful here every moment of the day. The excitement begins every morning at breakfast with the unfolding of "The Peking Gazette." I come down-stairs early, when the corridors are being swept and dusted by the China-boys in their long blue coats, and receive a series of "Morning, Missy's" on my way to the breakfast-room, the nice, warm breakfast-room, with oilcloth-covered floor, and everything else simple accordingly. There is gilding in the big dining-room, but the breakfast-room is as simple as a New England boarding-house. One boy pulls out my chair, another opens my napkin,—they look after you well here,—and a third boy, the regular waiter, leans over and says, "Pollidge, Missy?" and a moment later brings a big bowl of porridge and a can of cream. There is nothing but tinned milk and cream in China, for there are no cows. There is no room to pasture cows or to feed them, for one cow can eat as much food as twenty people, so no land can be devoted to such superfluities as that. One of the legations has a cow, however, and people who stand in well with the legation can have such milk as there may be over and above the legation's needs. But the Wagons-Lits Hotel is not on that list, and, as I say, tinned cream is all that I get for my "pollidge." But it is very good indeed, these chilly October mornings. After all, what does food matter? Peking is so rich in other things!

To-day at breakfast, with the "Gazette" propped against the coffee-pot, I began my usual search for news. Found it, too, in a moment, in the editorial column. A fairly long leader, entitled, "The Shanghai Opium Combine: Frantic Efforts to Secure Further Privileges in China," caused me to forget "pollidge" and everything else, and to read hastily to the end. As I told you the other day, the opium traffic in China is to come to an end in six months. Well, this article says that the Shanghai Opium Combine, the combination of a dozen British firms with headquarters in Shanghai, is making frantic efforts to prolong the time limit for the sale of opium, to extend it for another nine months. The excuse offered is that the combine has not sufficient time between this and April 1, 1917, to sell off its remaining stocks of opium, and in consequence it is appealing to the British authorities to bring pressure upon the Chinese Government to extend the time by nine months. According to the "Gazette," the combine has "worked hard to induce the local British consul-general once more to enlist his sympathies for the Opium combine; but, happily, the latter has peremptorily declined to do anything of the sort. It is reliably reported that the British Minister at Peking, Sir John Jordan, was similarly approached, and the latter has equally refused to recognize the combine any longer. As a last resort, they telegraphed to the London Foreign Office for support, in their desire to compel either the Chinese Government or the local Municipal Council [at Shanghai] to aid them to secure their nine-months' privilege. The decision of the London Foreign Office is awaited with feverish interest, although it is considered doubtful whether any good result can be achieved."

Think of China's position—having to await with "feverish interest" the decision of the British Government as to whether or not it will be possible for China to suppress the opium traffic at the end of the ten-years' agreement! The sale and manufacture of opium is a monopoly of the British Government, just as vodka was a monopoly of the Russian Government at the beginning of the war. The Shanghai Opium Combine is the distributing agent of this British opium, and until the beginning of this ten-years' struggle China was an important customer. The loss of revenue to the British Government through the closure of the Chinese market is a very serious item. And these rumblings, these hints of pressure being brought to bear upon China, are pretty ugly. Anyway, the "Gazette" is aroused to the danger, and the "Gazette" is nothing if not outspoken, and will give the matter full publicity if anything goes wrong. Only it makes one uneasy. Poor old China!

We went on such a pleasant expedition today. It was arranged last night on receipt of an informal note from Dr. Reinsch, our minister, asking if we would go with him on a donkey-trip to a temple in the hills outside Peking. Out came our khaki clothes, bought for just such an emergency, for nothing is more appropriate for a donkey-ride than our khaki skirts and breeches and leggings.

There are two railway stations in Peking, usually spoken of as "the station" and "the other station." From "the station" trains run down to Shanghai or up into Manchuria and Mukden, and connect with the Trans-Siberian and other far-away, thrilling places. The "other station" takes one out into the country somewhere, to various outlying spots in the hills, and it was to one of these places that we were bound. When we arrived we found the other members of the party waiting for us. We were all early, ahead of time, for Chinese trains have certain idiosyncrasies that must be reckoned with. Scheduled to start at a certain hour, they frequently leave five or ten minutes ahead of time, or whenever the guard thinks that no more people are coming. All six of our party found ourselves at the station well ahead of time, having been warned of this peculiarity of Chinese railways. Dr. Reinsch's two servants were on hand to buy the tickets and to carry large and imposing lunch-baskets. Soon we were all installed in an antiquated railway-carriage, first class by courtesy only, with half an hour's ride before us.

Pandemonium greeted us when we alighted on the platform of a dusty little station—a small house solitary upon the vast plain. Pandemonium came from the donkey-drivers who were expecting us, thirty or forty at least, each one dragging forward a reluctant donkey, praising its merits and himself as donkey-driver, and disparaging all the other donkeys and drivers and battling for our helpless persons. What can you do when a towering coolie takes a firm clutch on your arm, and, with an equally firm grip on his donkey's bridle, drags you and the donkey together and is about to lift you on the animal's back, when you are suddenly jerked in an opposite direction by an equally firm hand and confront another stubborn and reluctant donkey and are about to be boosted upon that, when you are clutched from the rear and meet a third possibility! Mercifully, our khaki clothes were new and strong and stood the jerking and hauling without giving way at a single seam. Out of the mêlée peace was finally restored. Some one got me, and the others also were captured, the yells finally died down, and we set off over the plains, all mounted on donkeys much too small. Saddles? Not at all. A square seat, about as wide and unyielding as a table-top, was strapped securely to each donkey, and to this seat we clung, with no secureness at all. An exceedingly wide seat it was, with stirrups dangling somewhere out of reach, and which could not be reached even by the widest effort to straddle that square wide pad. Behind each donkey ran its owner, flicking its heels with a long-lashed whip, urging it to a speed likely to pitch one off at any minute.

Do you think donkeys are sure-footed? I had thought so up to this time. By no means. These little beasts stumbled constantly, their little ankles having been so strained by the heavy burdens they ordinarily carry that they seemed to give way at every step. We had eleven miles of this, over a rough, uneven road, across the dusty plain, mounting gradually toward the hills through loose and rolling stones. It was a gray day, with rain threatening, and when we finally reached our temple, Je Tai Ssu, the rain began in a steady drizzle, and steadily continued.

The temple was most interesting. We stiffly rolled off our donkeys, and wandered through the multitude of courtyards, in and out of the many buildings, filled with fine carving and beautiful color. A few priests were at hand, deferential but unobtrusive, and when we finally sat down to lunch at a big table placed in the courtyard before the main temple, they surrounded us silently, filled with curiosity. The boys had placed our table under a tree, which did something, but not much, to shelter us from the rain that fell during the meal, dripping through the bare branches. Below us spread a magnificent vista of more hills, a great, far-reaching panorama, with the old Summer Palace in the distance. In all directions we could see temples perching on the distant hills—temples which are no longer used as such but are the summer homes of the foreign residents of Peking. They were all pointed out to us. Over yonder was Mr. So-and-So's temple; beyond, on that hilltop, was Mrs. So-and-So's, all occupied during the summer months by foreigners who escape from Peking in the hot weather. At once we became fired with a desire to rent one, too. Thirty Mexican dollars a season, a hundred Mexican dollars a year; not exorbitant, surely!

Besides the priests, the pariah dogs, or "wonks," watched our meal with intense interest. They stood by in a silent circle, monks and wonks, and our gay tiffin proceeded undisturbed except by the pattering rain. But the rain was increasing in violence, so we left soon after the meal, and it was far from easy to straddle our donkeys again and retrace our way across the stones and sand. From time to time we dismounted and tried to walk, but it was difficult to keep pace with our galloping animals, eager to return home. Time was pressing, so we were finally obliged to ride, becoming stiffer and sorer every minute. In single file as we had come, we made our way back. Presently I heard a sort of flumping sound behind me, and I turned, to see E—— and her donkey lying side by side in the road, motionless. Dr. Reinsch jumped off his animal, I rolled off mine, and we both ran back to the bundles of khaki and fur lying together at full length.

"Are you hurt?" I asked anxiously.

"Mercy no!" replied E——, contentedly. "Leave me alone! Most comfortable position I 've been in all day!"

VIII

ADVISERS AND ADVICE

THERE is another quaint custom here, which, as far as I know, is unique in the history of international relations. That is the custom of giving advice to China. Any country can do it, apparently. Any country that thinks China would be benefited by a little disinterested and helpful counsel can see that she gets it—and that she pays for it, too. Any person who wishes a lucrative position can get his government to appoint him as an "adviser" to China, and his government will see to it that China pays him a salary. As far as I know, China does not ask for this advice; it is thrust upon her unsought. But she must pay for the privilege, whether she likes it or not. So over they come, these various "advisers" from various foreign nations, and settle down here in Peking as the official adviser of this and that, and draw their salaries from this bankrupt old government. The China Year Book for 1916 gives a list of twenty-five such advisers, British, American, French, Russian, Dutch, German, Italian, Japanese, Danish, Belgian, and Swedish. There is the political adviser to the President; to the ministry of finance; in connection with the five-power loan; to the ministry of war; on police matters; to the ministry of communications; legal advice; advice on the preparation of the constitution; advice to the bureau of forestry, and to the mining department of the ministry of agriculture and commerce. In addition to all this paid "advice," there is of course the unpaid, voluntary "advice," equally disinterested and helpful, of the various foreign legations in Peking. No wonder the poor old Chinese Government is distraught and, as some one said last evening, in a state of anarchy. Who would n't be in the circumstances? I wonder how long Washington would tolerate such a string of "advisers," all appointed willy-nilly, and paid for by the American Government. They say that some one once wrote a book entitled, "Advising China to Death," but it was never published. Some one advised against it, probably.

Another thing that China is not allowed to do is to regulate her customs duties. This poor old country, rich as she is or as she might become, has virtually no revenue, for she is allowed to have but a nominal tariff. There is no use in developing her industries, she can't protect them, or hedge them in with any sort of protective tariff. It is not allowed. She must first consult with some seventeen different powers if she wishes to raise the duty on a single item. And if one power that does not import a certain article into China is willing to have a duty laid on that article, this decision will not be agreeable to another power that imports a lot of it. So it goes. It is pretty hard to find seventeen powers all in accord. The great nations allow old China just enough revenue to return to them in the shape of Boxer indemnities; nothing more.

Oh, disabuse your mind of the fact that China is a sovereign state! She is bound hand

and foot, helpless, mortgaged up to the hilt. Every foreigner in China knows it, and the Chinese know it themselves only too well. It seems such a farce to give them the courtesy title of sovereignty. I don't think you realize, never having been in this country, what a farce it really is. I am not able to write you a learned book. All I can do is to write you these letters, which are surely devoid of all legal verbiage, because I don't know any. If I were a scholar, a student of international politics, I would wrap all my statements in fine, well-chosen language, quoting treaties and acts and agreements and all the rest of it, and you would n't know what it all meant. I can only give you the facts as they disclose themselves to me from day to day. I can also tell you that every one over here—all the foreigners I mean—laugh at China and ridicule her and make fun of her weak, corrupt government, of her inertia and helplessness, and think what she gets is good enough for her.

I grow so tired of all this talk about the corruptness of the Chinese! They are corrupt, all the officials, or the greater part of them. But you don't hear much about those who corrupt them. Why? Because it suits the great Western nations to keep this government in a state of weakness, of indecision, of susceptibility to bribes and threats; it makes China easier to control. The one ray of hope for China lies in the fact that there are so many foreign nations trying to gain control of her. One could do it, two could do it, three could do it, but a dozen! China plays off one greedy predatory power against another. One "adviser" arranges everything nicely in the interests of his country, and then what does the "corrupt" Chinese official do? Runs off and tattles it all to some other "adviser," whose interests will be damaged if the advice of Number One goes through. It is a tremendous game, each foreign power striving to cut the ground from under the next foreign power and to gain the ascendency for itself. Diplomatic Peking is a great, silent battle-ground; on the surface Oriental politeness and suave political courtesies but underneath a seething sea of strife.

The Chinese attitude toward all this reminds me of a story I heard long ago. Two negroes were discussing a negro girl.

"Trus' dat niggah?" said one; "trus' dat niggah? I would n't trus' her 'hind a corn-stalk!"

Yes, many of the Chinese are corrupt. They have their price. For example, the old palace in the Forbidden City is now a museum, holding one of the most superb collections of Chinese treasures in the world, all that remains from the imperial go-downs. This collection is not catalogued, however, and every few months the exhibits are changed and others substituted; for the collection is too large, they say, for everything to be kept on view at one time. At such times as the exhibits are changed, current Peking gossip has it, certain of the finest treasures disappear. They are said to find their way into the currents of trade, to enrich the museums of Europe and America. Put this down as you like, however, the conventional explanation for this is that the Chinese are so corrupt!

IX

CHINESE HOUSES

WE are really, seriously looking for a house in Peking, in which to set up a Peking cart, a white mule, a camel, and a Mongolian dog! That shows what the Orient does to one in a few short weeks, how it changes one's whole point of view. A month ago neither of us had any idea of staying in Peking for more than two or three weeks; we had intended to stop long enough to see the obvious things, temples and such, and then go down to the tropics for the winter. Now we are on the verge of giving up our trip to Angkor and of settling right here—I was almost going to say for life! And all in a few short weeks!

There is so much beauty and style in a Chinese house, and most of the people we know have them, and we are becoming tired of being "tourists." Let me describe these Chinese houses. Each "house" consists of anywhere from two to a hundred little separate one-story buildings, the whole collection inclosed by a stone wall, ten feet high, with broken glass on top. Within this compound, or surrounding and protecting wall, the various houses are arranged symmetrically in squares, built around courtyards that open into one another. They are laid off with beautiful balance, and the courtyards, large or small, are usually paved with stone. Sometimes trees are planted in them, or bridges and rock gardens and peony mountains are made. The finer and more numerous the houses, the more beautiful and elaborate the architecture of these separate, single buildings, the larger and more elaborate the courtyards, the more filled they are with trees, lilac-bushes, stone bridges, and other charming details. As one enters the compound, the building facing one is the residence of the mandarin himself. Back of it lies the house of his "number-one" wife, and back of that, each surrounded by its own courtyard, are the houses of his other wives and of the various members of his family. All are quite separate one from the other, yet all are connected by passages leading through moon-gates in the dividing walls, one courtyard opening into another in orderly, yet rather confusing, profusion. However, we are not looking for anything grand and imposing—a palace or the abode of some old mandarin. We know several people who live in such stately homes, but we shall be satisfied with a simpler house, consisting of fewer buildings and fewer courtyards.

Inside the compounds, these various separate buildings are divided by invisible partitions into "rooms." In the ceiling one sees arrangements by which a wall can be built in, a screen adjusted,—a big carved screen,—or some sort of partition erected by which the house can be further subdivided. These possibilities for subdivision, whether by elaborately carved woodwork or by simple paper screens, are described as rooms, whether partitioned off as such or left open as one big one. Therefore one rents one's house according to the number of rooms it may be divided into, whether the division is made or not. We find we cannot possibly live in a house of less than twelve rooms, or four by ordinary reckoning. One house (three rooms) for E——, one for me, one for a salon, one for the dining-room. This makes four rooms, European calculation, twelve according to Chinese, and leaves nothing for guest-rooms, trunk-rooms, a study, or anything of the kind. Therefore, all joking aside, a house of a hundred rooms might do for us nicely!

How lovely they are, these one-story stone houses, with their tiled roofs, red lacquered doors, fine, delicate carvings on the window-lattices, and all the rest of it! The floors are of stone, but foreigners have wooden floors laid down. The winters are bitter here, and before these Chinese houses can be made comfortable according to Western ideas, much must be done to them. Some foreigners put in glass windows in place of the thick, cottony paper windows of the Chinese. The paper windows shut out the cold, it is true, but, being opaque, they also shut out the sunlight. And how gorgeously they are furnished! Such ebony chairs, such wonderful carved tables! Now and then we meet some one who has picked up an old opium divan, a magnificent, huge bench of carved ebony, with marble seat and marble back, very deep, capable of holding two people lying crosswise at full length, with room for the smoker's table between them. Only, the opium tables have been dispensed with, and their place is taken by cushions of beautiful brocade, of rich embroidery, which add something of warmth and comfort to the enormous couch. Mind you, all this furniture can be bought very cheap. To live Chinese fashion is not expensive at all, despite the impression of magnificence and luxury, which is rather overwhelming. When one considers that the most ordinary Chinese things are sold in America at a profit of three or four hundred per cent., the outlay for Chinese furniture in Peking is not great.

As to heating, stoves do it. Every room—I mean every one of these separate buildings—

is heated by its stove; a good big one, too. Russian stoves are found here and there, and any one who possesses a Russian stove is well equipped to withstand the bitterest winter. Now and then open fireplaces are introduced, but the big stoves go on functioning just the same.

These Chinese houses are charming from the outside. You wind your way along a narrow, unpaved street, or *hutung,*—a street full of little open-air shops, cook-shops, stalls of various kinds, and then come upon a high, blank wall, with a pair of stone lions at the gateway and an enormous red lacquer gate, heavily barred, and that 's your house. The gateman opens to your ring, and as the big doors swing back you see nothing of the courtyard or of the houses within the inclosure; you are confronted by the devil screen, a high stone wall about fifteen feet long and ten feet high. This devil screen blocks the evil spirits that fly in when the compound gates are opened—the blind evil spirits, that can fly only in straight paths, and hence crash against the devil screen when they enter. As to yourself, the gateman leads you round the screen, and across the compound to the master's house. Along the compound wall that gives on the street are the servants' quarters, the house for the rickshaws, the stables for the big mules and the Peking carts, and the house of the gateman. Life is none too secure in these compounds. Robbers abound, and scale the walls, and slip from the roofs of adjacent buildings into the compounds. Every household is in a constant state of alertness, of defense. Broken glass covers the tops of the walls, and in the courtyards Mongolian watch-dogs guard the premises, huge, fierce, long-haired creatures, like a woolly mastiff. Through the day they are chained, but at night they are unloosed. Oh, there is not only style but excitement in living in a native house in Peking! We have looked at a good many Chinese houses, but can't quite make up our minds about renting one. If we decide to stay, it will mean that we must give up our trip to Angkor, and it was to make that trip that we came out to the Orient!

Not every foreigner lives in a Chinese house, however. There are a few European ones, scattered about the Tartar City, looking so out of place, so insignificant and ugly! The foreigners who live here a long time seem to like them, however. They tell us that after a time China gets on one's nerves. Chinese things become utterly distasteful, and one becomes so sick of Chinese art and architecture and furniture that one must approximate a home like those of one's own country. Therefore there are a certain number of these "foreign-style" houses to be found, furnished with golden oak furniture, ugly and commonplace to a degree. I don't know how a long residence in Peking would affect us. At present we are too newly arrived, too enthusiastic, to feel any sympathy with this point of view. Let me add that when a foreign-style house is furnished with a few Chinese articles tucked in a background of mission furniture, the result is disastrous. One lady we met, who possesses such a house, recognized the humor of the situation.

Entrance gate to compound of Chinese house

Compound of Chinese house

"I know," she explained; "it 's just Eurasian."

We are undecided. If we take a house and settle down, we must give up our nice, warm little rooms at the old Wagons-Lits, forgo all the amusing gossip of the lobby, told in such frankness by the interesting people who know things, or think they do. They say housekeeping is not difficult here. You engage a "number-one boy," who engages the rest of the servants, and any one of the servants who finds himself overworked engages as many more servants as he may require; but that is not your lookout. The compound is full of retainers, and the kitchen as well, but you don't have to pay for them. They eat you out of house and home, squeeze you at every possible point, but add an air of the picturesque and of prosperity to the establishment. Housekeeping here is a throw-back to the Middle Ages, with a baronial hall filled with feudal retainers. And all for the price, except for the "squeeze," of one servant in America!

X

HOW IT 'S DONE IN CHINA

WE have got to Peking at just the right moment—right for us, that is, but one of the wrong moments for poor old China. These cycles of Cathay, I may mention, are filled with such moments for China, and this is just another of the long series, another of the occasions on which she is plundered. Only here we are, by the greatest of luck, to see how it 's done. Could anything have been more fortunate? Wait; I 'll tell you about it. You will hardly believe it. We should not have been able to believe it, either, if it had not taken place under our very noses.

Day before yesterday four of us went up to see the Ming tombs and the Great Wall. Everything is so exciting in Peking that we could hardly bear to absent ourselves from it even for two days; but, having come all the way out to China, it seemed as if we really ought to see the Great Wall. I won't describe our trip. You can read descriptions of the wall in any book; all I can say is that it took two days to get there and back, and that we set off on the expedition most reluctantly. E——'s theory is that it's best to get all the sights crossed off as soon as possible, so that we can enjoy ourselves with a clear mind. I had a presentiment that something would go wrong if we left Peking for such a long time, left China alone to her fate, as it were, for forty-eight hours. But E—— and the others thought this was as good a time as any, so in spite of our misgivings, we took advantage of what seemed like a quiet moment and slipped off on our excursion, to get it over with.

When we returned on Monday afternoon, we found the whole place rocking with excitement, boiling with rage and resentment, simply seething with fury and indignation. The hotel was ablaze. The moment we pushed open the big front door and entered—tired, dusty, and very shabby in our khaki clothes—

we were pounced upon and asked what we thought of it. Thought of what? Well, *this.* Night before last—the 19th of October, to be exact—the French had grabbed three hundred and thirty-three acres in the heart of Tientsin. The attack, or charge, or party of occupation, whatever you choose to call it, was led in person by the French chargé d'affaires, at the head of a band of French soldiers. They seized and arrested all the Chinese soldiers on duty in the district, put them in prison, and in the name of the Republic of France annexed three hundred and thirty-three acres of Chinese soil to the overseas dominion of the great republic!

Let me explain what this means. Tientsin is a large city, nearly as large as Peking, with about a million inhabitants. It is only two hours distant from Peking, by rail, and is the most important seaport of North China,—the port of Peking. Until the railway was built, a few years ago, the only way to reach Peking (other than by a long overland journey) was to come to Tientsin by boat, and thence to Peking by cart or chair. In spite of the new railway, Tientsin still retains its old importance as the seaport for North China, and is a trade center of the first rank. To seize three hundred and thirty-three acres in such an important city as this, was an act of no small significance. The annexed land, containing wharfage, streets, houses, shops, and the revenue from such, makes a goodly haul. Really, from the French point of view, it was a neat, thrifty stroke of business, or of diplomacy, or of international politics, whatever you choose to call it.

But from the Chinese point of view it is different. How are they taking it, the Chinese? How are they behaving? Well, in spite of the fact that the East is East and the West is West, that the Chinese are nothing but a yellow race and heathen at that, their feelings and reactions seem very similar to what I imagine ours would be in similar circumstances—I mean, if France should suddenly "claim" and "annex" three hundred and thirty-three acres of ground in the heart of Boston or New York. Their newspapers have broken out into flaring head-lines an inch high, and are wild in their denunciations of what they term an outrage; an infamous, high-handed act, a wanton, deliberate theft of territory from a peaceful and friendly country. Really, these Chinese newspapers seem to be describing the business in much the same words, with much the same force and fury and resentment, as our American papers probably would employ in describing such an episode if it took place in some American city. Only, our head-lines would probably be a little larger. However, the Chinese newspapers do very well, and what type they have seems to convey their meaning—rage and indignation. Mass meetings of protest against this outrage are being held in Peking, in Tientsin, in all the provinces, in fact; the governors of the different provinces are sending in telegrams; societies and organizations are telegraphing to the Peking government; the whole country is wild with resentment and is sending delegations and messages and protests to the poor old wabbly Chinese Government, urging it to "act." To act; that is, to tell the French

Government to hand back to China this "acquired" land. What the outcome will be, I don't know. Apparently the supine, terror-stricken Chinese Government cannot act, does n't dare. Three days have now passed, and the French are still sitting tight, holding to their fruits of victory, facing an enraged but helpless country. And they will probably continue to sit tight till the matter blows over.

I was eager to find out what constituted the French claim to this particular piece of territory, called Lao Hsi Kai. The French already possess a large concession in Tientsin, and why they should have wished to enlarge it, particularly in such a summary manner, I was anxious to discover. Their excuse is this: they asked for this Lao Hsi Kai area as long ago as 1902. That 's all. Asked for it years ago, and have been "claiming" it ever since. Have been asking for it at intervals during all these years. When the first request was made, in 1902, the ruling official in Tientsin considered it so insolent that he tore up the note and threw it into the scrap-basket, disdaining a reply.

Since then, whenever the request has been repeated, the Chinese Government has played for time, has deferred the answer, delayed the decision, shilly-shallied, avoided the issue by every means. This is the classic custom of the Chinese when confronted with an unpleasant decision,—to play for time, to postpone the inevitable, in the vain hope that something will turn up meanwhile, some new condition arise to divert the attention of the "powers that prey." Occasionally this method works but not always. Not in this case, anyway. When a European power asks for a thing, it is merely asserting its divine right.

We have talked to many people about this Lao Hsi Kai business, people of all ranks and all nationalities—diplomats, old residents, journalists, business men—and not one of them has made any attempt to justify or defend the action. Without exception, they say it is an outrage, and totally unwarranted,—at the very least, a most shocking political blunder. None of them, however, has come forward to the aid of the Chinese. A curious conspiracy of silence seems to reign,—not silence in one sense, for every one is talking freely with most undiplomatic candor, and in private every one condemns what France has done, yet not a voice is raised in public protest. The Chinese alone are doing their own protesting; and much good it seems to do them!

XI

THE LAO-HSI-KAI OUTRAGE

A WEEK has passed since the French "acquired" Lao Hsi Kai, and the situation remains unchanged. The French still sit tight, waiting for the storm to blow over; the Chinese continue to hold their protest meetings, to send in their delegations and requests to the central government to act; the government sits supine, afraid to budge; and the newspapers continue to rave. It is all most interesting. The "Gazette" devotes almost its entire eight pages to what it calls the "OUTRAGE" and has n't decreased the size of its type one bit. If it had larger letters, it would probably use them. I should think that by this time, after such long and painful experience with foreign powers, it would have laid in a stock suitable to such occasions.

The "Gazette" is an annoying sort of newspaper,—annoying, that is, to the powers that prey. Under the caption "Madness or War," in the biggest head-lines it has, it insists upon describing this Lao Hsi Kai affair as the most Belgium-like thing that has happened since the invasion of Belgium. Alike in principle, if not in extent. Whipped up into a white heat of fury, it draws, over and over again, the most disconcerting parallels.

And all this week it has continued to be irritating, referring constantly to Belgium, and harping upon the Allies' ideals,—the preservation of civilization, liberty, justice, and the rights of small, weak nations. The "Gazette" insists that these ideals should be applied to China, forgetting, apparently, that while China is weak, she is not small!

Meanwhile, at the mass meetings which are being held all over the country, especially at Tientsin, the officials are trying to calm the people. It is feared that some violent action will take place, some hostile demonstration against the French which will throw the Chinese entirely in the wrong, no matter how great the provocation. If this happens, the sympathy of the world will be turned against the Chinese, and the officials are striving by all means to prevent such an outbreak. A quaint account of one of these indignation meetings was published in one of the Peking papers:

On Saturday morning more than four thousand merchants and inhabitants of Tientsin gathered themselves at the Chamber of Commerce at Tientsin, declaring that as the French authorities had disregarded international law and principle, they would devise means themselves for the preservation of their own liberty against the aggression of foreigners. The Chairman of the Chamber came out with the representatives of the Society for the Preservation of National Territory to appease the indignation of the public, and to persuade them not to resort to violence, but to seek a constitutional method to arrive at a peaceful solution through the proper channels. He at once proceeded with the people to the office of the Shengcheng, who said, "The Frenchmen are indeed most aggressive and unreasonable. Your humble servant is ready to sacrifice position, rank, even life itself, for the preservation of the territory of the nation. A telegram has already been sent to the Central Government giving a detailed report of what has happened here, and a reply will soon be received giving instructions for our guidance." The Chairman of the Chamber of Commerce replied: "I am afraid that the people are out of patience now, and there are several thousands of merchants and other classes of people awaiting instruction, outside your office. It would be advisable for you to come out and pacify them, informing them what you would do." When the Shengcheng came out, the audience clapped their hands and shouted at the top of their voice. Some even wept, and others cried "Liberty or Death" and suchlike expressions. The Shengcheng said: "I am also of your opinion. I will sacrifice my life, too, for the maintenance of the territory entrusted to me for preservation. And I can assure you that no foreigner shall be allowed to occupy one inch of our territory in this unreasonable manner."

It is pitiful to read these accounts and the telegrams sent to the President of China and to Parliament, and to realize that the weak and cowed government at Peking cannot defend itself against the foreign aggressor. However, the Chinese people have taken affairs into their own hands, to a certain extent, and have organized a run on the French bank, the Banque Industrielle de Chine. One of the branches of this bank is around the corner from the hotel, and all day long, for the past several days, a long, patient line of Chinese have been standing, waiting to withdraw their accounts from the bank of the country which has treated them so ill. This run on the bank, conducted by a huge crowd of quiet, orderly men and women, is a favorite Chinese method of retaliation. They say the bank is losing enormous sums in consequence, is obliged to buy great quantities of silver to maintain its credit. Also, there are rumors flying about that a boycott of French goods is shortly to be established.

The attitude of the English newspapers (those that represent the foreign point of view) is illuminating. They are laying all these manifestations of resentment to "agitators," refusing to believe in the indignation of the people themselves. Every day the newspapers representing the foreign interests are becoming more and more abusive. Here is one extract that seems particularly insulting:

> The Chinese agitator, particularly if he believes that he enjoys official support, is invariably willing to fight to the death for some cause that he professes

to have at heart, until there is some risk that he may be taken at his word. Then he invariably beats an ignominious retreat. And unless we are greatly mistaken, this is what will happen in this case. We are familiar with the normal course of events—public and press clamor, attempts to institute a boycott, and finally, when the Power whose interests are affected, intimates that it has had enough of this tomfoolery—collapse of the whole agitation. . . . If the French Legation, after allowing sufficient time for the self-styled patriots to let off steam, intimates that this nonsense has got to cease, the great crusade for the protection of China's sovereign rights over fifteen hundred mow [three hundred and thirty-three acres] of land formally promised to the French authorities several months ago, will collapse as suddenly as it began. Whenever a crisis in China's foreign affairs occurs, we are treated in the Chinese press to humorous dissertations about Chinese dignity and self-respect. How such things can exist, even in the Chinese imagination, at the present moment, passes comprehension. The China of to-day cannot seriously expect much respect or consideration for her dignity from foreign states, because these things are only accorded to nations that are worthy of them.

Read this paragraph over and ponder it well. It appeared in an English newspaper, the semi-official organ of the European point of view. There is nothing veiled or hidden in the attitude of the dominant race!

XII

THE LAO-HSI-KAI AFFAIR

ANOTHER week has gone by, the atmosphere is still tense and surcharged with feeling, and the situation remains unaltered. However, the newspapers have changed their headings from "Outrage" to "Affair," although they are still devoting columns and columns to the matter. Protest meetings are still being held, and the run on the French bank must have been pretty successful, from the Chinese point of view, for there is now talk of an indemnity for the damage done! Listen!

Already Threats of Indemnity. The French Consul at Tientsin is already threatening to demand damages. He contends that the Tientsin people should not be allowed to hold a meeting of protest against what is clearly an outrage on the integrity of China. He says the Chinese authorities are guilty of the "violation of treaty rights" and therefore must be held responsible for any damage done to French commerce. The French Consul also objected to the presence of officials [Chinese] at the meeting, but omitted to state that the local officials did their best to calm the people and persuade them to wait patiently for the decision of the Government.

Well, I have always wondered how it was that poor old China is forever paying indemnities, first to one country, then to another; I have never known how it came about. Pretty easy, come to think of it! First grab a piece of Chinese soil, then suppress all protests by levying an indemnity.

The "Gazette" seems to have gone too far in its championship of China, and has got into trouble. Almost from the beginning the editor has insisted that the French Government itself was not to blame for this affair. He has asserted repeatedly that this high-handed procedure was the individual action of the French consul-general. As far as I can see, these little "affairs" always take place in the absence of the minister,—a well-timed vacation, during which an irresponsible chargé d'affaires acts on his own initiative. Be that as it may, on this occasion the French minister happens to be in Paris, and the "Gazette" is insisting that the chargé d'affaires has exceeded his authority and acted without instructions. Apparently this interpretation is given partly because of a desire not to involve the two governments in a hopeless snarl admitting of no retreat, and partly to calm the rising anger of the Chinese, who are incensed at the delay in restoring the captured land. While stoutly refusing to retire from its position as the champion of Chinese liberty and territory, the "Gazette" is insistent that this act could not have been committed at the instigation of a country at present fighting for liberty and justice, a great nation pledged to noble ideals.

Whether this attitude has been due to a sincere belief in the Allies' professed ideals, or whether by the fixing of blame on an irresponsible official who has exceeded his authority, the French are being offered a loophole to retreat from an intenable position without "losing face," I don't know. Certain it is that "justice, liberty, and civilization" have been dragged into the argument, day after day, with irritating persistency. Really, the Oriental mind, plus contact with a higher civilization, was becoming unbearable. So a stop was put to it in this way: One morning the papers contained an announcement that "The Allied and neutral ministers despatched an identical note to the Chinese Foreign Office, warning the Chinese Government against allowing the Chinese press to attack the diplomatic body in the way it had lately done, and practically demanding that the Government take some steps to prevent the attempted raising of anti-foreign feeling."

Is n't it lucky we are here at this moment! Could you believe it! Now you know how "indemnities" are raised, and how "anti-foreign feeling" is aroused. A day or two afterward, a further pronouncement was made:

> Comments in the Chinese press have been rather rude and sharp, so that the Ministry [Chinese] has been requested by the British, Russian, French and Japanese and other foreign governments to caution the editors and proprietors of Chinese papers to

exercise more care and discretion in their recording of foreign intercourse affairs, and that sufficient politeness should be showed to foreign ministers and consuls as a sign of courtesy toward the representatives of Treaty Powers in this country.

There you have it—the Chinese press muzzled at the instigation of foreign powers! Since that happened a few days ago, I have n't got nearly as much fun out of my "Gazette" in the morning when I have had my "pollidge." But, thank Heaven, the English newspapers, representing the interests of the foreign powers, are able to spout freely. And these papers have been having a wonderful time describing the happenings in Tientsin, where the threatened boycott has gone into effect. For the Chinese, baffled in their attempt to regain their captured territory, have instituted what they call that "revenge which must take the form of civilized retaliation, namely, refusal to buy or sell French goods." On an appointed day there was a general walk-out in the French concession in Tientsin. All the Chinese in French employ—house servants, waiters, electricians in the power-houses, stall-holders in the markets, policemen, every one in any way connected with or in French service—took themselves off. Moving-picture shows are in darkness; interpreters and clerks in banks and commercial houses have disappeared; cooks, coolies and coachmen have departed; and life in the whole French concession is entirely disorganized! The French consul-general sent a letter of protest to the Chinese Commissioner of Foreign Affairs, calling for "strict preventive measures on the part of the Chinese authorities," and the answer of the Commissioner, the prompt and polite reply, was to the effect that the only preventive measure for these disturbances would be to hand Lao Hsi Kai back to the Chinese!

How demoralizing this boycott is may be gathered from the way the foreign press is raging about it. One bitter editorial, entitled, "A Plain Talk to the Chinese," has this to say:

> Boycotts and strikes, in lieu of diplomatic action, are becoming somewhat of a fad with the Chinese. They have been practised with impunity and consid-

erable success for the past fifteen or twenty years. . . . We wish to impress upon the Chinese people and Government that these anti-foreign agitations are becoming somewhat of a nuisance, and it is high time the foreign powers stepped in and put a stop to them. . . . The foreign powers have no means of getting directly after this handful of agitators, but they have the means and the power—the will only is necessary—to hold the Chinese Government responsible, and to demand satisfaction in full for all losses suffered by firms and individuals as a result of these organized boycotts. We wish to warn the Chinese that this boycott business can be carried out once too often, and it looks to us that they have just now reached this once-too-often stage. If the French Government, backed up by the Allies, demands indemnity for all losses sustained, we will hear the last of Lao Hsi Kai and all similar affairs in China. It may be just as well to remind the Chinese Government, in case they conclude that the Allies are too busy in Europe to pay serious attention to Chinese affairs, that the Japanese are one of the Allies, and *their* hands are not particularly tied at present.

Good gracious! A threat to call in the Japanese! Don't you love it!

XIII

THE LAO-HSI-KAI "INCIDENT"

IT 'S about over, I should say. The French are going to keep their ill-gotten gains, and the Chinese are giving up all hope of getting Lao Hsi Kai back again. The thing has drifted from an "Outrage" into an "Affair" and now it 's only an "Incident," which means it 's over. The boycott continues, but it is dwindling in intensity and will soon subside. It is now but a question of time before China settles down to an acceptance of the situation, bows before the might and majesty of Western civilization, and prepares herself for the next outcropping of kindred ideals.

You ask, why did n't the Chinese fight? "What with, stupid Gretchen?" How can a virtually bankrupt nation like China take up arms, which she does n't possess, against the mighty nations of Europe? Defenseless, unarmed China is no match for the "civilization" of the West!

A few nights ago I got a French point of view of the affair, and will give it to you just as I heard it, without comment. One of the attachés of the French legation was dining with us. This Lao Hsi Kai business, which has been uppermost in every one's thoughts for the last four weeks, was naturally in our minds as we sat down at dinner. Not to mention it would have savored of constraint; yet it was equally embarrassing to speak of it. After ten or fifteen minutes, during which the subject was carefully avoided, I took the bull by the horns.

"Seems to me you 've stirred up a great mess out here," I began.

"Mess?" replied the young Frenchman. "Oh, you mean that affair of the other day! Ah, these Chinese! Perfectly impossible people!"

He crumbled his bread a while, and then continued with much heat.

"For fourteen years," he burst out, "we have

been wanting that piece of land, and asking for it! Asked them for it fourteen years ago! Told them fourteen years ago that we wanted it!

"And what did they do?" he went on irritably. "What did they do but procrastinate, knowing we wanted it! Put us off. Postponed a decision. Practically refused to give it to us, knowing we wanted it! Other things came up in the meantime, so we did not press them, and the matter dropped for a number of years. However, we took it up again in 1914, two years ago. It was the same thing—procrastination; delay; no positive answer. Then we pressed them a little harder. What did they do? Asked for more time to think it over, more time after all these years, knowing we wanted it! Knowing that we had asked for it fourteen years ago, as far back as 1902! Knowing that we had asked for it as far back as 1902, they still had the audacity to ask for more time to think it over!

"However," he resumed, "we gave them more time. They asked for a year. We gave them a year. When the year was up, they asked for six months. We gave them six months. When the six months were up, they asked for three months. We gave them three months. We were most reasonable and patient. When the three months were up, they asked for one month. We had infinite patience. When the one month was up, they asked for two weeks. We gave them two weeks. We had infinite forbearance. Think of it! Naturally, at the end of two weeks, when they still had not made up their minds, we took it. What else could we have done? We had given them every opportunity, for fourteen years. Ah, these Chinese! They are impossible. No one can understand them!"

We are going to leave Peking within a day or two and go down to the tropics for the winter. This is the end of November and it is getting bitterly cold, and with the on-coming of cold weather we seem to have reverted suddenly to our original plan of visiting Angkor. So you will get no more Chinese letters from me until the spring, when we are planning to return to Peking. It has all been most exciting, most interesting, but we are thoroughly tired out with having our sympathies so played upon, so wrought up, and feeling ourselves impotent. It is distressing to stand by and see such things transpire under our very eyes, injustices which we are powerless to prevent. I shall be anxious to know whether anything of this affair has crept into our American papers. I suppose not, however. We are anxious only to see "civilization" triumph in Europe. The backwash of civilization in the Orient is not our concern. All I can say is this: The world would have rung with news of such a grab if Japan had been guilty of it.

PART II

I

THE RETURN TO PEKING

WE have been away now for three months, and it seems like getting home, to be back in our beloved Peking. We reached the shabby old station, the other evening, worn out from the long two-days' journey up from Shanghai, and it was good to have the porter from the Wagons-Lits greet us and welcome us like old friends. It was pleasant to walk back along the long platform of the station, under the Water Gate, and to find ourselves, in a minute or two, in the warm, bright lobby of this precious hotel. The doorkeeper knew us; the clerks at the desk knew us; and the various "boys," both in the dining-room and up-stairs in our corridor, all knew us and greeted us with what seemed to our tired souls real and satisfying cordiality. "Missy way long time. Glad Missy back," "Missy like Peking best?" And Missy certainly does. Moreover, if you have once lived in Peking, if you have ever stayed here long enough to fall under the charm and interest of this splendid barbaric capital, if you have once seen the temples and glorious monuments of Chili, all other parts of China seem dull and second rate. We began here, you see. If we had begun at the other end,—landed at Shanghai, for instance, and worked our way northward,—we should probably have been enthusiastic over the lesser towns. But we began at the top; and when you have seen the best there is, everything else is anticlimax.

We arrived the other evening in a tremendous dust-storm, the first real dust-storm we have experienced. We ran into it at Tientsin, where we changed trains to continue the last two hours of our journey north, and were uncomfortable beyond description. The Tientsin train was absolutely unheated, cold as a barn. The piercing wind from the plains penetrated every nook and crevice of the carriage, and the cracks were legion: the windows leaked, the closed ventilators overhead leaked, the doors at each end of the carriage leaked, and we wrapped ourselves in our ulsters and traveling-rugs and sat huddled up, miserable and shivering. But it was n't wind alone that blew in through the numerous holes. There was wind, of course, in plenty, but it carried in it a soft, powdery red dust, a fine, thin dust, able as the wind that bore it to sift through every crack and opening. It filled the carriage, it filled the compartment, and when the lamps were lit we sat as in a fog, dimly able to see each other through the thick, hazy atmosphere. There we sat, coughing and sputtering, breathing dust into ourselves at every breath, unable to escape. We became covered with it; it piled itself upon us in little ridges and piles; no one moved much, for that shook it off into the surcharged air, already thick enough, Heaven knows.

Two hours of this, bitter cold and insufferable, choking dust. And every one in the crowded compartment was suffering from Chinese colds; we had them too, contracted at Shanghai. And let me tell you that a Chinese cold is something out of the ordinary. Whatever happens here happens on a grand scale, and these colds, whatever the germ that causes them, are more venomous than anything you 've ever known. No wonder the railway station looked good to us; no wonder we were glad to be welcomed back to the old hotel, at the end of such a journey!

We found plenty of hot water when we got here. Not that hot water does one much good in Peking. For Peking water is hard and alkaline, and about as difficult to wash in as sea-water, if one uses soap; we are dirty despite all the facilities afforded us. I should say that the Chinese had given up the struggle several generations ago; and small blame to them. We reached here the last day of February, and are now experiencing a taste of real Northern winter, just the tail of it but sufficient. Coming up from the Equator, as we have done, the shock is rather awful. This winter, they say, has been an extraordinarily severe one, even for Peking, where it is always cold; they tell us it has been the coldest winter within the memory of the oldest foreign resident. I don't believe much in these superlative statements, however: people always make them concerning hot or cold weather, in any climate or in any country. However, the thermometer went so low on several occasions that the pipes burst, and the hotel was without heat; very trying with the weather at twenty below zero. Nevertheless, in spite of the lingering cold, in spite of the dust, in spite of the hard water and other discomforts, Peking is the most delightful place in the world, not even excepting Paris, than which, as an American, I can say no more.

We have been here a week now, have recovered from our Chinese colds, and are getting hold of things again. We are catching up with all the gossip, all the rumors, all the *dessous* of Chinese politics, which are such fun. And just as I expected, too, it was n't safe for us to go away, to leave China to flounder along without us. Things have happened in our absence: I won't say that we could have prevented them, but at least we could have been on the spot to take notes. That is what makes Peking so absorbing,—the peculiar protective feeling that it gives one. In a way it seems to belong to us; its interests are our interests; its well-being is peculiarly *our* concern. You wish the best to happen to China, you wish Chinese interests to have the right of way. And whatever you can do to promote such interests, however small and humble your part may be in advancing them, it is your part nevertheless, and the obligation to fulfil it rests upon you with overwhelming insistence. As I told you before, China is overrun with "advisers." Consequently we all feel ourselves "advisers," more or less, all capable of giving advice just as worthless or just as valuable as, certainly more disinterested than, that which the Chinese Government is compelled to pay for. Everything is in such a mess here—so anarchic, so chaotic—that you feel you must put out a hand to steady this rocking old edifice; and you also feel that your hand is as

Chinese funeral

Chinese funeral

strong, and probably as honest, as the next one.

In no other country that I know of do you feel so keenly this sense of possession, this wish to protect. The other countries belong to themselves, absolutely. For example, Japan owns itself and directs itself; the Japanese don't let you know much about what 's going on in their country; and you feel that it is none of your business anyway. They are quite capable of managing their own affairs. So in Europe: the affairs of the European peoples are their affairs, not your concern at all. But the case is so different with poor, weak, helpless China. China enlists all your sympathies, calls forth every decent instinct you possess.

For these are dark, distressful days for China. At present she is passing through a reconstruction period corresponding to our reconstruction period after the Civil War. Just five years ago the revolution occurred by which she rid herself of the Manchu rulers, an alien race which had dominated her and ruled her for two hundred years. And chaos followed that upheaval, just as political chaos followed the close of our Civil War. We, however, were free to work our way upward and outward from the difficulties that beset us at that time, out of the maze of corruption and intrigue that almost overwhelmed us. We were permitted to manage our own affairs, to bring order out of that chaos, harmony out of strife, without having to deal with foreign predatory powers who for their own ends were anxious to prolong the period of internal dissension. China is not free in that respect: not only must she set her house in order, but she must deal with those foreign powers who do not wish her house in order, who are slily and adroitly using their enormous, subtle influence to defeat this end. During our reconstruction period in America we made mistakes; but after those mistakes we did not have to hear a chorus from European nations telling us that we were unfit to govern ourselves. Nor were we forced to have other nations trying to corrupt every honest man we wished to put in office, nor to have these alien nations attempting to put into power dishonest and inefficient men as their own tools. That is China's problem at present: not only must she contend against the inherent weakness and dishonesty, the inefficiency and graft of her own people, but she must contend against unseen, suave enemies, who under diplomatic disguise are intriguing to bring the nation under foreign control.

I have not been able to get much definite news so far. Our Chinese colds proved so severe that they were nearly our undoing. I fancied myself reposing under a little mound on the plains, after an imposing Chinese funeral. I must say I should have enjoyed a Chinese funeral, with drums and horns, flags and banners, carried along in a car supported by three score bearers. But for the present it 's not to be.

II

THE OPIUM SCANDAL

I KNEW it would happen. I knew that if we went away from Peking for even a short time, let alone for three months, something would take place that ought n't to. The minute you turn your head the other way, take your hand off the throttle, pop goes the weasel! It 's popped this time with an awful bang. The papers are full of it, pages and pages, the entire paper, and not only one or two but all of them. You have probably not been permitted to hear a word of it at home, but the Chinese papers are allowed to explode all they please, to rail and rave and rant. As I said before, much good may it do them.

I wrote you last autumn of the ten-year contract entered into between China and the British Government, the final outcome of the contract to be the total suppression of the opium trade. Every year for ten years the importation of British opium into China was to decrease in proportion to the decrease of native-grown Chinese opium, until at the expiration of the ten years the vanishing-point would be reached. During these ten years each side has lived up to its part of the bargain. British imports have been lessened year by year, scrupulously, and the Chinese have rigidly supervised and suppressed the production of native opium. China began to plant poppies extensively after 1858, the year in which Great Britain forced the opium trade upon her.

The ten-year contract was to expire on April 1, 1917, a day which the Chinese press referred to as "a glorious day for China and her well-wishers throughout the world, a day on which a nation liberated herself from an age-long vice." I also told you last autumn something of the activities of the Shanghai Opium Combine, a combination of several firms of British opium-dealers, who were making prodigious efforts to have the time limit extended. This Shanghai Opium Combine are not officials of the British Government: they are private firms, private dealers; but they buy their opium direct from the British Government, and may therefore be considered its unofficial agents or middlemen. This Opium Combine had been appealing for an extension of the ten-year contract, an extension of nine months. They had appealed to the various British officials in China, and to the Foreign Office in London, but apparently the British Government had turned a deaf ear to these pleas, which must have been a hard thing to do, considering the enormous revenue that country derives from her opium monopoly. Even without the Chinese markets, one would have supposed that the markets of India, Siam, the Straits Settlements, etc., and other subject or helpless states, would afford these dealers opportunity to get rid of their surplus stocks. But no. The opium was in China, in their go-downs in Shanghai, and they wanted nine months' additional time in which to get rid of it.

If this time extension had once been granted, however, pressure would have been brought to bear at the end of the nine months for a further extension; and so on, and so on, upon various pretexts. Accordingly, the British Government refused to interfere in the matter, and very honorably decided that the opium traffic in China was to end on the date specified, April 1, 1917.

But what did the Shanghai Combine do? Finding they could not sell their remaining chests of opium before the first of April (which they could easily have done had they not held them at such exorbitant prices), they apparently "influenced" the Vice-President of China to purchase them in behalf of the Chinese Government! There were some three thousand of these chests, each one containing about a hundred and forty pounds of opium, and the sum which the Vice-President pledged China to pay for this opium was twenty million dollars. China was under no obligation whatsoever to purchase this. In a few more weeks the contract would have expired, and China would have been automatically freed. The Shanghai Combine could either have disposed of their chests at reasonable prices within the time limit, or else hawked them round to other markets. But, the Vice-President having been "influenced" in this manner, this well-nigh bankrupt country is now about to issue domestic bonds to the value of twenty million dollars to pay for this indebtedness.

This secret treaty, this dastardly betrayal of China by her Vice-president and the British opium-dealers, is apparently a one-man deal. After the contract between them was signed, Parliament and the country at large was notified of the transaction, and once more the country is ablaze with indignation. Once more mass meetings of protest are being held throughout the provinces; telegrams from governors and officials are pouring in; the contract is denounced and repudiated by Parliament; but all to no purpose. This infamous contract holds and cannot be broken. China must pay out twenty millions of dollars for this drug, which she has made a superhuman strug-

Courtesy of Far Eastern Bureau

Vice-President Feng Kuo-Chang

View of Peking, looking north, towards Forbidden and Imperial Cities

gle to get rid of. And as twenty millions is a sum far in excess of the real value of these three thousand chests, the papers are freely hinting that Baron Feng was bribed.

Feng's excuse is that he was obliged to conclude this deal for "diplomatic reasons." You can draw your own conclusions as to what that implies. He also says that it was better for China to buy these chests outright than to have them smuggled in later. Also he says the Chinese Government can now sell this opium at discretion, in small amounts, for "medical purposes." Legitimately to dispose of three thousand chests of opium for medical purposes, would require about five hundred years.

By reason of this infamous deal China is now faced with the probable resumption of the opium traffic. The Chinese Government has become, like the British Government, a dealer in opium. It must dispose of this opium either for "medical purposes" or for smoking purposes. This will undoubtedly mean that poppy cultivation will again be resumed. It is not inconceivable that the same sinister pressure which was brought to bear upon the Vice-president may also be brought to bear upon planters in the interior provinces, should they be unwilling, which is unlikely, to raise once more these profitable crops. And if China goes back to poppy cultivation, Great Britain may feel at liberty to import opium again. If that happens, the whole vicious circle will be complete. All barriers will be down, and this whole long, ten-years' struggle will have been in vain.

The whole country is shocked, appalled, dismayed. No one sees any way out of this *impasse.* One suggestion is made that this opium be destroyed, a bonfire made of it. It would be a costly proceeding, for this almost bankrupt nation cannot afford to destroy twenty million dollars with a wave of the hand. We can only wait and see what the outcome will be. Only once can a drug-sodden nation rise to grapple with such a habit as this. Only once can a nation set itself such a colossal task. The fight was made against great odds, under a tremendous handicap. But it was carried on in the belief that at the end of ten years the fight would be won. If betrayal is to be the outcome of such a mighty effort, what incentive is there to begin again, to renew the struggle, should things slip back to the conditions of ten years ago? The country is overwhelmed with disappointment and humiliation. No one knows what the future holds in store. The great nations of the world stand silent, in this hour of China's betrayal.[1]

[1] See Appendix I.

III

THE WALRUS AND THE CARPENTER

WE have got back to China just in time to witness another interesting event. The decision has now been reached that the time has come for China to go to war. She has been "notified" to this effect. What she will eventually do is the question. Anyway, the screws are now being put on in earnest: you can fairly hear them creaking.

As I wrote you in one of my letters last autumn, ever since the outbreak of the war numerous but vain efforts have been made from time to time to draw China in. Inducements of various kinds have been offered her during these last two years, but she has resolutely turned a deaf ear to these overtures and remained neutral. But the time has now come when her resources and her man power are needed; consequently the screws are turning gently but relentlessly, and China is being crowded along into a realization of her duty toward civilization.

Wilson's note to China, asking her to break off diplomatic relations with Germany, was similar to the notes he despatched to the other neutral countries, asking them to do the same thing. In the case of China, however, it gives the Allies the opportunity they have been looking for, and they have all sprung forward in a chorus of endorsement. They have been unable, for obvious reasons, to make much of an appeal on the score of high morality: the Orient is not quite the ground in which to sow seed of that kind, especially after Lao Hsi Kai and the recent opium deal. But America's record in the Far East is well-nigh irreproachable, and when we ask China to join with us—

So the papers are discussing the question back and forth, from every angle, for and against, with every shade of frankness, bitterness, enthusiasm, and doubt. There are those who would trust America utterly: we have always been China's friend, sincerely and disinterestedly; we would not lure her into a disastrous adventure. There are others who distrust the predatory powers, and who are frankly puzzled at our joining them. They question our motives. Are we going to pull them up to our level, to our high idealism, or are we going to sink to theirs? The Oriental mind is an old, old mind, richly stored with experience and memories,—not in the least gullible and immature. Therefore, they very earnestly desire to know. America has never deceived them, never played them false. But —but—what does it all mean? They cannot be sure.

This is no fertile field for crass, popular propaganda. On the one hand the Allies urging China to join with them. On the other hand America, their friend. This great country sways back and forth between them, very much puzzled.

So the papers discuss the affair freely, frantically, copiously, favorably and unfavorably, and one wonders what the outcome will be.

The first step, of course, is to induce China to break diplomatic relations with Germany. After that the next step, naturally, will be a declaration of war. So high is feeling running, that they freely prophesy that this will split the country wide open, into civil war. If China could get rid of all her European masters at one fell swoop, well and good. But she hesitates to pack off one enemy, and surrender herself hard and fast into the keeping of the rival group.

Here let me tell you of a doctrine that seems to be making much headway in the Orient: we have come across it over and over again, in varying circumstances. That is the doctrine of Pan-Asianism, or Asia for the Asiatics. Logical enough, come to think of it. The Monroe Doctrine for Asia, in which the Orientals shall govern and own themselves, and not be subject to the control and guidance, however benevolent, of Europe. They argue that Oriental control of Europe would be hotly and bitterly resented; and they are prepared to resent Occidental control of Asia. Do not dismiss this theory lightly. It is spreading more and more widely throughout Asia, and some day it will be a force to be reckoned with. Also, these Pan-Asians will tell you the contention that the Orientals cannot manage their own affairs is untenable. Japan is an example to the contrary. If the smallest and least of the countries of Asia has been able to do this, it is because she has *been let alone,*—not conquered, exploited, nor drugged.

Which reminds me of that poem in "Through the Looking Glass," called "The Walrus and the Carpenter." It will bear re-reading. The nations of the East have been playing the part of little oysters to the Walrus and the Carpenter, and the little oysters are having their eyes opened.

. . . .

"A loaf of bread," the Walrus said,
"Is what we chiefly need:
Pepper and vinegar besides
Are very good indeed—
Now if you 're ready, Oysters dear,
We can begin to feed."

"But not on us!" the Oysters cried,
Turning a little blue.
"After such kindness, that would be
A dismal thing to do!"
"The night is fine," the Walrus said.
"Do you admire the view?"

. . . .

"It seems a shame," the Walrus said,
"To play them such a trick.
After we 've brought them out so far,
And made them trot so quick!"
The Carpenter said nothing but
"The butter 's spread too thick!"

"I weep for you," the Walrus said:
"I deeply sympathize."
With sobs and tears he sorted out
Those of the largest size,
Holding his pocket-handkerchief
Before his streaming eyes.

"O Oysters," said the Carpenter,
"You 've had a pleasant run!
Shall we be trotting home again?"
But answer came there none—
And this was scarcely odd, because
They 'd eaten every one.

"I like the Walrus best," said Alice: "because he was a *little* sorry for the poor oysters."

"He ate more than the Carpenter, though," said Tweedledee. "You see he held his handkerchief in front, so that the Carpenter could n't count: contrariwise."

"That was mean!" Alice said indignantly. "Then I like the Carpenter best—if he did n't eat so many as the Walrus."

"But he ate as many as he could get," said Tweedledum.

IV

CHINA'S COURSE CLEAR

CHINA has sent a note of protest to Germany, under date of February 9. It was a dignified note, but, somehow, one could almost see the mailed fist guiding the slim, aristocratic, bony hand that penned it; the delicate, sensitive hand, with long finger nails; the weak hand of China.

To His Excellency von Hintze, Envoy Extraordinary and Minister Plenipotentiary of Germany.

Your Excellency: A telegraphic communication has been received from the Chinese Minister at Berlin, transmitting a note from the German Government dated February 1, 1917, which makes known that the measures of blockade newly adopted by the Government of Germany will, from that day, endanger neutral merchant vessels navigating in certain prescribed zones.

The new menace of submarine warfare inaugurated by Germany, imperilling the lives and property of Chinese citizens to even greater extent than measures previously taken which have already cost so many human lives to China, constitute a violation of the principles of public international law at present in force; the tolerance of their application would have as a result the introduction into international law of arbitrary principles incompatible with even legitimate commercial intercourse between neutral states, and between neutral states and belligerent powers.

The Chinese Government, therefore, protests energetically to the Imperial German Government against the measures proclaimed on February 1, and sincerely hopes that with a view to respecting the rights of neutral states and to maintaining the friendly relations between these two countries, the said measures will not be carried out.

In case, contrary to its expectations, its protest be ineffectual, the Government of the Chinese Republic will be constrained, to its profound regret, to sever the diplomatic relations at present existing between the two countries. It is unnecessary to add that the attitude of the Chinese Government has been dictated purely by the desire to further the cause of the world's peace and by the maintenance of the sanctity of international law.

Well, well, thinks I, on reading that note, wonders will never cease! Is this the same China, prating about the sanctity of international law, that sat supine and helpless under the French grab of Lao Hsi Kai? Is this the same China that accepted the deal of the Shanghai Opium Combine, powerless to prevent it? How comes it that she 's got this sudden influx of moral strength? Who or what has suddenly inspired her to make these bold assertions about "arbitrary principles incompatible with even legitimate commercial intercourse," and what pressure is it that suddenly inspires her to step into the arena as the champion of "world's peace" and the defender of the "sanctity of international law"?

Besides the note to Germany, China transmitted a note to the United States. This was addressed to Dr. Paul S. Reinsch, American Minister, etc., to Peking:

> Your Excellency: I have the honor to acknowledge the receipt of Your Excellency's Note of the 4th of February, 1917, informing me that the Government of the United States of America, in view of the adoption by the German Government of its new policy of submarine warfare on the 1st February, has decided to take certain action which it judges necessary as regards Germany.

The Chinese Government, like the President of the United States of America, is reluctant to believe that the German Government will actually carry into execution those measures which imperil the lives and property of citizens of neutral countries and jeopardize the commerce, even legitimate, between neutrals as well as between neutrals and belligerents, and which tend, if allowed to be enforced without opposition, to introduce a new principle into public international law.

The Chinese Government, being in accord with the principles set forth in Your Excellency's Note, and firmly associating itself with the Government of the United States of America, has taken similar action by protesting energetically to the German Government against the new measures of blockade. The Chinese Government also proposes to take such action in future as will be deemed necessary for the maintenance and principles of international law.

Again I marveled at the lofty tone of this note, and wondered how this moral strength had been so suddenly acquired. Thought I to myself, can this be poor old browbeaten China,—humbled and prostrate before the powers of Europe, unable to protest when her territory is snatched away from her,—now suddenly giving voice to these exalted ideas?

Does it not seem rather ludicrous that she should suddenly proclaim herself the upholder of international law? Like Moses of old, she is now stretching forth her arms; but who are they who uphold those arms? These solemn notes are given forth to the world, and the world is asked to believe sincerely, as China herself states, that they were "dictated purely by the desire to further the cause of the world's peace and by the maintenance of the sanctity of international law." Let us believe it, if we can.

An editorial in the "Shanghai Times," a British paper, under the date of February 12 throws some light upon the matter. The article is entitled "China's Course Clear"; the italics are mine.

To those of us who live in this corner of the Far East, a question of paramount importance is the attitude which the Republic of China is likely to take up in regard to the war. The pendulum of Fate may swing in our favor, and the Peking Government —acting on the counsels of its statesmen *and its friends*—may decide to unite its forces with the Allies. This is a question which interests us individually, it touches our daily lives, and becomes a theme of much discussion at a moment when neutrals are emphasizing to the Hun their rights and their insistence of Germany's recognition of these privileges. . . . Germans in Shanghai and possibly other ports are to-day existing on the instalments which are being paid as Boxer Indemnity. *The Germans have big interests up north in railway and other enterprises; they penetrated the Customs and captured positions in other Government circles. There is a great deal at stake in China.*

This frank and lucid statement contains food for thought. It may possibly lie at the root of China's sudden acquisition of moral strength. It is true that the Japanese have acquired Shan-tung since the war, but there are "big interests up north in railway and other enterprises" which have not yet been captured. Fat plums which may yet be shaken into some expectant lap. But will the Chinese, in spite of their ample skirts, have laps wide enough to catch them? Would it not be well to see that these ripe plums do not fall into the lap of Chinese incompetence?

The Lord knows.

V

FEAR OF THE PLUNGE

CHINA is now wavering on the brink. Having despatched her two notes, and thereby proclaimed herself worthy to rank as a first-class power, with a seat at the Peace Table promised her, and all the benefits which accrue therefrom, she still hesitates to make the break. Unquestionably several of her officials and other prominent men have already succumbed to what the papers call "foreign influence," lured by the words of spellbinders, but there are others who are stoutly resisting all appeals, and who see in such a step dire calamity for the country. The fact that China has no real reason to break with Germany makes the decision more difficult. A plausible excuse of some kind must be offered the country, and such flimsy pretexts as the necessity of upholding the sanctity of international law are difficult to get away with. The Chinese press is full of the incongruity of the situation, and outspoken of its amusement.

Besides keeping the Lao Hsi Kai affair constantly before the people, it is relentless in its denunciation of Vice-President Feng's opium deal, and the methods of the British opium-dealers. Columns in regard to this transaction are published every day in the papers, throwing light on some new phase of it, keeping the public constantly informed regarding it, and asking the people at large to consider well the advisability of allying themselves with such friends as the French and English have proved within the last few months. Thus, in regard to the opium deal we read:

High Official Offered Bribe of $5,000,000. A report is current in the Capital that some time ago, a man representing himself as the Manager of the Shanghai Opium Combine, approached a certain high official and solicited his good offices in consummating the opium transaction, which is now being carried out by the Vice President. According to the paper, the man promised the high official five million dollars as a "birthday present," a euphemistic term for bribery in this country, if the Combine, through his influence, succeeded in concluding a deal with the Government. The attempt fell through because the high official is too honest to be thus corrupted. Finding the authorities in Peking incorruptible, the Combine turned its attention to Nanking.

Nanking being the residence of Baron Feng.

It is very interesting to watch this struggle, to see the various forces at work. The passions of the Chinese are being played upon: the public is constantly reminded of the insults and indignities that China has suffered at the hands of those nations who are now urging her to join with them. The people are not allowed to forget it is through force and bribery that China has been reduced to her present plight; they are asked to be skeptical of promises made by those nations who employ such methods. It is having its effect, too, this press campaign. While the foreign diplomats are working upon a handful of officials, the people are being reminded of the wrongs they have suffered through the machinations of these diplomats, representing predatory powers.

But, after all, the Chinese people, four hundred millions of them, are a negligible quantity. The ultimate decision rests with a dozen high officials. It simply remains to influence these officials, and the thing is done. They are of three types: those, like the Vice-president, open to direct bribery; those, like the premier, Tuan Chi jui, who have political ambitions and whose ambitions can be played upon (they say Tuan wishes to become president); and certain others, of the younger school, who are dazzled by the promises made to China and are unable to offset these promises with the experience of years. These last rejoice to think that China has been promised a seat at the Peace Table, which means that China is recognized as a first-class power. All sorts of inducements are offered, including cancelation of the Boxer indemnity now being paid to Germany. (The Allies have very obligingly decided that payment of their own Boxer indemnities shall be postponed, not canceled.) Also, there are vague, indefinite hints afloat to the effect that if China is very, very good, the Allies will consider, kindly consider, the right of China to raise her customs-duties. She may, perhaps, be allowed some sort of protective tariff. This latter hint is very vague indeed, too nebulous, in fact, to have much weight. But, after all, the cancelation of the German indemnity is something.

The disadvantages, on the other hand, are these: If China enters the war, she must equip her armies. Being virtually bankrupt, she must first borrow. From whom? She must mortgage herself again, to somebody, before she can borrow money to equip her armies. And will the country from whom she borrows money, who agrees to train and equip her armies, also have full military control over the affairs of China? Will that nation be given liberty to suppress her press, to stifle all opposition to whatever moves military necessity may dictate? It looks like complete surrender.

But the Chinese are not blind, not all of them. Nor are they all corruptible. And very few of them have utter, childlike faith in the motives of the Allies..

VI

A DUST-STORM

S—— INVITED us to go with him to the Gymkana at the race-course.

"It 's a rather amusing sight," he explained. "You 'll see all foreign Peking scrambled together out there." Then he went on: "Take the special train from the 'other station,' and, when you arrive, follow the crowd to the club-house. I 'm riding out from town, so may possibly be a minute or two late, though I expect to be on hand to welcome you when you arrive. But if I 'm a little late, please don't mind."

We assured him that we should n't mind at all; and then he went on to say that he hoped we 'd have a pleasant day and no dust.

These dust-storms are the curse of Peking and of North China. To-day, however (March 5), dawned bright and clear and sunny, as usual; but clear, bright weather is not necessarily the sign of a fine day in this part of the world. Not in spring. Every day is one of brilliant sunshine, the winter sunshine of China just south of the Great Wall, and just south of the Mongolian desert. That 's where the dust comes from. It blows in straight from the Gobi Desert, and makes the late winter and the spring, particularly the spring, almost intolerable. Since our return we have been having dust-storms on an average of twice a week, big ones and little ones, lasting from a few hours to several days. There are two kinds: surface storms, when a tremendous wind blows dense clouds of fine, sharp dust along the streets and makes all outdoors intolerable; and overhead storms, which are another thing. These latter really are a curious phenomenon: fine, red, powdery dust is whirled upward into the higher levels of the atmosphere, blown overhead by the upper air currents, from which it drifts down, covering everything in sight. On such occasions there is frequently no wind at all on the streets, but the air is so filled with dust that the sun appears as in a fog, a red disk showing dimly through the thick, dense atmosphere. The dust floats downward and sifts indoors through every crack and crevice, until everything lies under a soft red blanket. You simply breathe dust for days; there is no possibility of escape until the wind changes and it is over.

To-day, however, apparently was going to be a good day. I ran down the hotel corridor to look at the flags flying over the legation quarter, the flags of most of the nations of the world. The sight was reassuring. No wind at all, apparently; they were all idly flapping from their poles, whereas yesterday they had been frantically tearing at them, whipped out stiff by a piercing, cold north wind. So we took rickshaws and were soon running along toward the Hankow station, where we found a large crowd of foreigners assembling for the special train that was to take us to Pao Ma Tchang, literally "Run Horse Place," the race-course six miles from Peking.

When we dismounted, we had the usual arguments with the coolies as to fares. There are three classes of fares here,—one for the Chinese, one for the sophisticated resident, and one for the tourist; each one double that for the preceding class. By this time we consider ourselves sufficiently at home to pay the tariff which the foreign residents pay, sufficiently sophisticated to avoid being overcharged. No use. We never seem able to manage it. Inside of a minute we had half the coolies of Peking yelling round us, just as if we were the greenest tourists that ever set foot on Chinese soil. I 'm sorry for the rickshaw boys, they have a hard life of it; yet I must confess that our sympathies are somewhat alienated by the way they "do" us on every possible occasion.

The special was waiting in the station, and we installed ourselves in a compartment and looked eagerly out upon the platform for the signs of the "scrambling" we had come to see. There it was, too, all the Who 's Who of Peking,—all the ministers and secretaries of the legations, with their families and guests, and all the foreign residents of the legation quarter and the East City and the West City and every city contained within the walls of the capital. Americans, English, French, Danes, Russians, Swedes; only the Germans were absent. The railway pierces the wall of the West City, and for a time we ran along under the walls outside, with the great crenelated battlements rising above us, and their magnificent gates or towers glittering in the sunshine. How incongruous and insignificant seemed that train-load of chattering foreigners beneath the majestic, towering ramparts of this old royal city! The arid plains presented rather a Biblical appearance, with camel-trains moving slowly across the desolate landscape, while here and there flocks of broad-tailed sheep were browsing, tended by their shepherds. We passed the usual graves,—little mounds of earth ploughed round very closely, as closely as the people felt they might without disturbing the spirits within.

Twenty minutes later we came to a stop on the plains, and every one began getting off. In a moment we were surrounded by crowds of yelling donkey-boys leading donkeys, and a few rickshaw-pullers as well. No one seemed to care for either form of conveyance, and we soon left behind the blue-coated coolies still shouting the merits of their tiny gray donkeys with their tinkling bells, and began a journey on foot across the dusty plain. Road there was none: merely an ill-defined track presented itself, along which all the ministers and secretaries of the great nations of the world walked, ankle-deep in dust.

But something had gone wrong with the weather. Our pleasant day, on which we had staked our hopes, had somehow disappeared. We had noticed, as the train moved along, that clouds of dust seemed to be rising; but we laid this to the speed of the train, fully twelve miles an hour. But once outside the shelter of our carriage, it was impossible to deceive ourselves any longer. The wind was rising, and the dry dust of many rainless months was rising with it, flying in dense, enveloping clouds. It was a curious sight that presented itself: a long, straggling procession of two or three hundred men and women, beating their way, heads downward, across the plains of Chili in what turned out to be a dust-storm of colossal proportions. Presently the Chinese band passed us, its members mounted on donkeys, galloping by with their drums and horns bumping up and down behind them. We were glad when they disappeared over a knoll on the horizon.

We finally reached the club-house, a simple, unpretentious little building, with wide, open verandas in front, which afforded no shelter from the biting wind. The whole procession staggered in, a choking, coughing, sputtering crowd, and from one end of the line to the other rose imprecations on the weather, in every language known to Europe. As E—— and I stood there, beating the dust off our clothes and looking for some sign of S——, one of the foreign ministers came up to us, raising an immaculate gray hat, in sharp contrast to a very dusty overcoat. "Have you an invitation to tiffin?" he asked, as he shook hands. We hastily said we had, were expecting our host any minute. We don't know what his intentions were. These are war times, and Peking is surging with furious suspicions. He may have meant to ask us to lunch with him, or he may have meant to put us out as intruders. Fortunately, at that minute S—— appeared round the corner, wiping his face and eyes; he claimed us and all was well.

Two or three races were to be run before tiffin, and we went out to have a look at the ponies, little Mongolian ponies with short, clipped hair. They were the same breed as the shaggy little animals one sees everywhere in Peking. E—— and I know nothing of horses; there 's no use pretending. But in spite of that blinding dust, every one else was attempting to distinguish the various points, good and bad, of the snorting, struggling little beasts, who were as unhappy about the weather as we were. And between you and me, I think it was a fine affectation to pretend to distinguish qualities in that storm. In the paddock racing-camels and donkeys also were tied up, and let me say I think it was all an honest person could do in the circumstances to tell the difference between a camel and a horse. Our interest centered in the camels, the great, disdainful camels, who looked down upon ministers plenipotentiary and potentates and powers with such superb hauteur. Really, these Peking camels are the aristocrats of the world; you feel it every time they condescend to glance at you.

The wind, which was getting higher and colder every moment, soon drove all but the most ardent enthusiasts indoors. We mounted to the upper story of the club-house, and looked out over the course from the windows of the big dining-room, which occupies the entire upper floor. Before us stretched the same bleak, arid plains that we had crossed on our way from the station: only the railing marking the outer boundaries of the track divided it from the barren stretches of earth which extended northward to the uttermost confines of China. Not a blade of grass was anywhere in sight. And over all, the dust—not the ordinary dust of a windy March day at home, but great, thick, solid clouds of dust, reaching upward, and covering the entire sky. The noon sun gleamed down in a circle of hazy red.

There were two races before lunch. One could n't see the ponies till they were within a hundred yards of the winning-post. S——, who has great courage, and moreover felt his responsibility as host, would remain outside on the upper veranda, straining his eyes in the biting gale, and then signal to us when they came in sight. Whereupon we would rush outdoors for a brief moment, clinging to our hats and groping for the veranda rail, and stand there for an agonizing minute till he told us it was over.

Now and then, in brief pauses in the wind, the horizon would clear for a moment and we could see beyond the outer boundaries of the course. We caught occasional glimpses of long caravans of camels, two or three hundred of them, bound for the coal-mines up north. Once, in a short interval, we saw a funeral procession stretching away over the plains—a straggling procession on foot, in dingy white dresses, carrying banners and flags and parasols. The coffin was slung on a pole between bearers, and the wailing drone of a horn, and the thud of a big drum came down the wind. Then the dust rose again, and the melancholy sight was shut out. How curious was this little pleasure spot of the Europeans, in the midst of this barbaric setting, in the heart of old, old Asia!

Tiffin time. Every one who had not already taken refuge in the dining-room now trooped up-stairs, hungry and laughing. I must tell you of the dining-room. It was just a huge, square, bare room, with whitewashed walls, with not a picture, with not an attempt at decoration. A dozen trestle tables ran across it, with narrow, backless benches on each side,—benches which had to be stepped over before one could sit down. Every one stepped over them, however—ministers and first-secretaries and Russian princesses and smart American women; and you had to step over them again when the meal was finished, too, unless by some preconcerted agreement every one rose at the same time. There was not a chair in the place. Every one was dust-grimed, wind-blown and bedraggled, and it was a gay, noisy meal, with laughter and cigarette smoke and dust all through it.

In spite of the noise, however, there seemed little real merriment. One became conscious of the atmosphere,—of the forced, rather strained, I was going to say hostile, atmosphere. Every nation, as if by prearrangement, withdrew to itself. The English sat together, the French sat together; the Russians were apart; and the Americans in still another section. There was no real intermingling, no real camaraderie, except among the individual groups. There was much hand-shaking of course, and greetings and perfunctory politeness, but no genuine friendliness. The various ministers, for instance, did not sit together as ministers, off on a holiday. On the contrary, each one sat at the table with his countrymen. Over all there was a feeling of constraint, distrust, national antipathies but thinly veiled, with but the merest superficial pretense of disguising intense dislikes and jealousies.

In Peking there is great freedom of speech, and much outspoken criticism of one nation by another; for there hatred and suspicions run high. Therefore, of course, such feelings could not be submerged on an occasion of this kind. Perhaps the war has intensified them; perhaps they are always there; perhaps this is the chronic atmosphere of Peking, where each power is trying to outdo the other, to overreach the other, in their dealings with China. Anyway, E—— and I were intensely aware of it in this "scrambling together" of all diplomatic Peking.

No Japanese was present, although a few Japanese are members of the club. And it is significant that no Chinese, no matter how high in rank, is admitted to membership. The impression we derived of this European playground is that the attempt to play is a farce. You look over your shoulder to behold a knife at your back.

After tiffin two more invisible races took

place, but no one made an attempt to see them. The dust sifted in through the windows and lay thick on the tables, and one made footprints in it on the floor. Then we were all cheered by the announcement that the special train was returning an hour earlier than the time scheduled, and there was a general move to go. The walk back across the plains was even worse, if possible, than that from the station to the club-house, for the wind was stronger, the dust more blinding. Yet the whole procession was light-hearted, somehow: there were prospects of a bath at the journey's end. As we reached the station the train was pulling in. E—— was walking just ahead of me, talking to the Russian minister, Prince K——. A gust more violent than usual struck us, and I saw her suddenly leap aboard while the train was moving. When I joined her a moment later she seemed rather dubious.

"I don't know that that 's exactly the way to take leave of a prince," she said doubtfully, "to jump on a moving train in the middle of a sentence."

VII

A BOWL OF PORRIDGE

WHILE we were at the races yesterday in all that dust, exciting things were happening in Peking. We no sooner returned to the hotel than there were a dozen people to tell us of them. It seems that at a cabinet meeting yesterday morning (March 5) the prime minister, Tuan Chi jui, wished to send a circular telegram to the governors of the various provinces announcing China's determination to sever diplomatic relations with Germany. The President of China, Li Yuan Hung, who is strongly opposed to this course, rejected the premier's proposal, whereupon Tuan tendered his resignation and flew off in a huff to Tientsin. Tuan is forever resigning his post as prime minister, and is forever being coaxed back. A deputation to coax him back was sent the day afterward, and there were those who hoped he would return and those who hoped he would n't. And now, a day or two later (March 7) back he comes and all is well. The problem, however, is still to be settled. Tuan is pretty powerful, has the backing of the military, and is said to be desirous of becoming president. It is all very complicated and difficult to understand, and there are rumors floating about that he departed not because the President refused to break with Germany but because his life was in danger. There was some plot on foot to assassinate him, and his suggestion concerning the telegram to the governors was merely an excuse for his resignation, for the necessity for quickly leaving Peking. Plots to assassinate people always occur at critical moments, and it is most uncomfortable for all concerned.

The papers are full of tales of coercion, of charges of bribery, of hints of pressure being brought to bear upon Chinese officials. China must be made to break with Germany and to do it soon. A few days ago we met an intelligent little Chinese lady, wife of an "official in waiting." (This is a nice title, and means an official waiting for a job.) She is an alert, well-educated, advanced little person, who has spent several years in America, and speaks English fluently with almost no accent. She is thoroughly conversant with the present political situation, too,—having doubtless discussed it with her husband, the official in waiting,—and was most outspoken concerning it. She grew very indignant as she spoke of the pressure being brought to bear upon China, and she told of a dinner recently given in Peking, given by certain foreign officials to certain Chinese officials whom they wished to "influence." When the plates were lifted, a check was found lying beneath each plate. She got so excited over this incident—as I did, too—that I forgot to ask her what the Chinese officials did with these checks.

"I should think you would hate all foreigners," I said. "I should, in your place."

"We do!" she replied emphatically, and her black eyes flashed. "Why don't you leave us alone?"

"Which of us do you hate most?" I asked, "or least?—if you like it better that way."

The Chinese have a delightful sense of humor, something that you can always count upon. She wrung her little claw-like hands together, twisted them with emotion; yet her sense of humor prevailed. She flashed a brilliant smile upon me.

"You Americans we hate least," she explained. "You have done the least harm to us. And some of you, individually, we like."

"But, naturally, you hate us all?"

"Why not?" she replied. "See what you foreigners are doing to us, have done to us, are still trying to do to us. Can you blame us? Judge for yourself."

"I can perfectly understand your Boxer uprising," I told her, "when you tried to get rid of us all—"

"I 'm glad you can understand that," she retorted. "Few foreigners do. We feel that way still; only we can't show it as we did then."

Into my mind came a recollection of the high stone wall surrounding the British legation, on which are painted the words, "Lest we forget." Every day, as one passes in or out of the legation quarter by that road, one's attention is arrested by those words. "Lest we forget." Every foreigner in Peking is thus reminded of those dreadful months of siege in 1900. But so is every Chinese of the upper classes; so is every rickshaw coolie who stops to point out those words to the tourists as he passes. Why remember? Why not try to forget? Neither side will forget. Neither foreigner nor Chinese has any intention of forgetting. The huge indemnities that are paid out year by year by the Chinese make forgetting impossible. Of all the countries that received an indemnity, America was the only one that tried to forget. Yet she did it by erecting a monument to her forgetfulness, or forgivingness, in the shape of a college-preparatory school for Chinese boys, and is using part of her yearly indemnity fund to maintain it; and "Lest we forget" is written large upon its walls.

But in contrast to the bitterness of the little Chinese lady, we received an impression to-day of quite opposite character. We called upon the editor of one of the Chinese papers. We have seen him many times, and he has often had tea with us in the lobby of our hotel, but upon this occasion he sent us a note and asked us to call on him at his office. He kept us waiting a few minutes in a shabby, dingy office, littered with papers and newspaper clippings, the regulation untidy office of a newspaper man. When he finally arrived, after ten minutes' delay, he apologized profusely, saying it was five o'clock, the hour for his bowl of porridge. He looked as if he needed it, too, for he was a thin, nervous little man, a burning, ardent soul contained in a gaunt, emaciated body.

Straightway, after his allusion to his porridge, he burst into a eulogy of America, such as it did our hearts good to hear. In his mind there was absolutely no question that China should trust herself to America, enter the war on the side of America. No other nation in the world, he said, had such great ideals, and so thoroughly lived up to them. Wilson's

Mexican policy filled him with enthusiasm; he spoke of it at length, almost with tears in his eyes. Next he touched on our Philippine possessions. Our record in the Philippines is an example to the world. No exploitation of a helpless people but a noble constructive policy to educate them, develop them, and, finally, bring them to a point where they could exercise their own sovereignty. The first thing we did, he reminded us, on taking possession of the Philippines, was to throw out opium. It was at that time a drug-sodden country, but our first act was to banish the traffic, root and branch.

It was also America, he went on, which had given China moral support and active backing in her ten-years' struggle against the drug. We had called together the Opium Conference at Shanghai, and later the Hague International Opium Conference, and owing to the publicity gained through these conferences China had had the courage to demand the opportunity to eradicate the curse. On and on he went, and it was good hearing. He would use his influence, and it was great, to induce China to accept America's invitation and enter the war on the side of the Allies.

It made one rather humble to hear him. China will place her fate and her fortunes so implicitly in our hands. It will be a great responsibility for us to meet. Do you think we can do so?

VIII

FROM A SCRAP-BOOK

THIS is n't a letter. I shall take a bunch of old newspapers and with scissors and paste-pot, stick upon this sheet of paper such press comments as seem relevant to the situation. First of all, remember that China has a population of four hundred million people, of whom three hundred and ninety-nine million have never heard of the European war. But the opinion of the million that may have heard of it is of no moment. The few people it is necessary to convert to a sympathetic understanding of the European war are the handful of officials composing the Cabinet, about two hundred members of Parliament, and a small, outlying fringe of "officials in waiting" and other odds and ends, generals and such like. Once convince them, and the thing is done. The understanding million, and the three hundred and ninety-nine millions who do not understand are negligible. At present there is a good deal of talk about restoring the monarchy. You don't have to deal with as many people in a monarchy as in a so-called republic. A monarchy is a more wieldy body. China, however, a five-year-old republic, is behaving just like any other democracy,—forever appealing to the people, as if the people even in a democracy had any chance against their masters and rulers.

Thus the "Peking Gazette," under date of Tuesday, March 1:

The Entente and China. Reported Allied Decision. A report reaches us—which we have been unable to confirm—that the Entente Ministers and Chargés d'Affaires in the capital met at the French Legation on Tuesday and considered the advisability of deputing the Japanese Chargé d'Affaires to call on the President, the Vice-President and the Premier, to ascertain the decision of the Chinese Government regarding further action against Germany. In the event of failure on the part of the Chinese Government to decide on the matter this week, the report adds that a joint Allied inquiry will follow next week.

In the absence of confirmation, we have to reserve comment on what looks like an amazing blunder, if true. In the meantime, we have to warn those concerned, that unless they are bent on alienating the growing Chinese sympathy for the Allied cause, and arresting the powerful movement for some form of action, in association with or in coöperation with the Entente, it will be well if anything like Allied pressure be avoided at this juncture.

Since writing the foregoing—or rather as we go to press—we learn from a responsible quarter that the French Minister and the Belgian Chargé d'Affaires called at the Chinese Foreign Office yesterday afternoon and either informally suggested or actually invited China to join the Entente. In the name of the Allies, they are understood to have promised the postponement of the instalments of the Boxer indemnities accruing due and payable during the war, and guaranteed the revision of the Chinese customs tariff. We have just time to register our emphatic protest against this proceeding; and limiting ourselves to the bare statement of one of the many grave objections to this action of the Entente, we have to point out that it is not real Chinese interest for the Allies to thrust large sums of money on persons who may not be able to apply the same to national ends. The Chinese Government is in need of money for specific objects, like the resumption of specie payment, the disbandment of superfluous troops, and the liquidation of certain unfunded indemnities. Financial assistance to the authorities is something for which the country would feel grateful to any Power or group of Powers who might render the same. But Chinese who have the real interest of their country at heart will not thank those who—without regard to the vital interest of China—are resolved upon securing the support of a few ambitious men whose single aim is to have enough money to influence, first, the Parliamentary elections, due in a few months, and next, the Presidential election to be held next year. Curses not blessings would issue from our lips for such questionable assistance to the forces of reaction in Peking.

On March 2 appears a translation from a vernacular paper, the "Shuntien Shih-Pao":

At a recent meeting of Allied Ministers in the French Legation, it was decided that if China does not declare her intention to join the Allied nations within the next few days, the Allied nations should give advice to China to that effect.

Apart from "advice" of this sort,—rather threatening advice, it would seem,—appeals are being made to Chinese vanity, by the contrasting of the potential might of China with the might of Japan. In an article entitled

"China and the World War," Putnam Weale, speaking for the British interests in China, makes some clever but rather blunt suggestions:

> So far, no one has gone beyond suggesting the general mobilization of Chinese labor-battalions, some of which are already at work on the Tigris building docks, and thereby contributing very materially to the vastly improved position in Mesopotamia. But it does not do credit to the stature of the Chinese giant, or to the qualities of the Chinese intellect, for Chinese to remain hewers of wood and drawers of water; it is imperative that if the nation goes to war she should actually fight, as the experience of the last five years shows what she can do with skill and science. In advancing the contention that a definite offer of a picked Chinese Division, or of several divisions, to Great Britain, against a definite treaty, to hasten the Mesopotamian campaign would be a master-stroke of policy, we have to recall that Japan herself refused to send contingents to the Balkans, and is therefore looked upon as a semi-belligerent whose stature can at once be overtopped by the Chinese giant merely rising to his feet.

A clipping from a Paris paper, the "Petit Parisien," has been reproduced in the Chinese press, and given prominence. The Chinese colossus is not asked to rise to its feet merely to demonstrate its huge proportions. If it rises, it must be to serve a purpose. With a simple frankness due perhaps to a failure to consider possible quotation in the Peking press, the "Petit Parisien" comments upon the "Value of China's Intervention" thus:

> The intervention of China is not to be underrated. The Chinese army at present is sufficiently instructed and equipped, well officered and supplied, and possesses large reserves. The military schools are in a position to train nearly five thousand officers a year, and this figure could be increased five times, if needed. The natural resources of China would enable her to supply raw materials for the ammunition and machinery, as well as leather, cotton, rice, tea, and other commodities.

In exchange for these natural resources, to develop which China will have to mortgage herself to the Allies, is offered cancelation of the Boxer indemnity to the Germans, and postponement (not cancelation) of the indemnities paid to the other nations. There are also, as I have said before, vague hints that China may be allowed to revise her tariffs and place a duty upon certain commodities. But even with the first suggestion of such tariff revision comes opposition, from Japan. The Allies, who have no cotton to import to China at the present moment, may generously consent to protective duties on this article, but Japan, which has plenty of it to import, objects to a handicap to her cotton-trade. If the Allies require China's intervention, then let them pay for it. Thus the "Chugwai Shogyo," a Japanese newspaper, under date of March 7:

Buying China's Friendship. We maintain that the Foreign Office [Japanese] officials should resolutely refuse to agree to the raising of the Chinese customs tariff. But it is reported that the officials are backing out. They are goody-goody people. They seem to think that the Chinese proposal is a just one. There is no reason why China should make any unjust claim. But even if China's claim is intrinsically just from her own standpoint, we should not agree to it if it is disadvantageous to us. Besides, if China makes that claim as her condition of her joining the Entente Powers, it is not right. If China thinks that to sever her relations with Germany and Austria is disadvantageous to her, and therefore wants to obtain a *quid pro quo* for so doing, this consideration should be given by the Entente Powers, not Japan. Is the participation in the war beneficial to China or to the Entente Powers? If the former, then China should not ask any compensation. If the latter, then the compensation should be paid by the Entente Powers, not Japan. From the point of view of Oriental peace, there is no absolute necessity for China to participate in the war.

Sun Yat Sen, the great revolutionary leader and spokesman for the more enlightened Chinese of South China and Canton, has also sprung into the arena, and makes a protest against dragging China into the war. In an open letter to the Prime Minister of England, which appeared in the papers under the date of March 7, he says:

To His Excellency Lloyd George, London.

Your Excellency: As a patriot of China and grateful friend of England, to whom I owe my life, I deem it my duty to point out to you the injurious consequences to China and England caused by this agitation of some of your officials here, to bring China into the European conflict. I have been approached by prominent English to consider the question of China joining the Allies. After careful study

I come to the conclusion that it would be disastrous to both countries should China break her neutrality.

For China is yet an infant Republic and as a nation she may be likened to a sick man just entering the hospital of constitutionalism. Unable to look after herself at this stage, she needs careful nursing and support. Therefore China cannot be regarded as an organized country. She is held intact only by custom and sentiment of a peace-loving people. But at once, should there arise discord, general anarchy would result.

Hitherto the Chinese possessed unbounded faith and assurance in the strength of England and her ultimate triumph, but since the agitation by short-sighted though well-meaning people, while some English dailies even advocate the sending of several Chinese divisions into Mesopotamia, this confidence has been greatly shaken.

Should China enter the war, it would prove dangerous to her national life and injurious to the prestige of England in the Far East. The mere desire to get China to join the Allies is to Chinese minds a confession of the Allies' inability to cope with Germany. Just now comes Premier Tuan's report to the President that the Entente Powers are coercing China to join the Allies. Already the question has raised bitter dissensions among our statesmen. Discord now may evoke anarchism which will arouse the two strong but perilous elements in China, anti-foreign fanatics and Mohammedans. Since our revolution, anti-foreign feelings have been suppressed by us, but anti-foreign spirit lives and may take advantage of the critical time and rise in another Boxer movement with general massacre of foreigners. If war is declared against any country, the ignorant class cannot distinguish one nation from another, and consequences would be more fatal to England, owing to her larger interest in the Orient.

Again, the Mohammedans cannot be overlooked. To fight against their Holy Land would be a sacrilege.

The worst results of anarchism in China, I fear, would be dissension among the Entente Group, which would surely mean disaster to the Entente cause. Under such conditions and at this critical juncture, China cannot be expected to do otherwise than maintain strict neutrality.

My motive for calling your Excellency's attention to this injurious agitation is actuated not purely by the desire to preserve China from anarchy and dissolution, but prompted by my warmest sympathy for a country whose interest I have deeply at heart, and whose integrity and fair name I have every reason to uphold and honor.

SUN YAT SEN.

IX

THE GERMAN REPLY

THE German Government has sent a reply to China's protest, a most conciliatory note, saying that it is extremely sorry to hear that China's shipping has suffered so greatly through the submarine warfare, and that if China had protested sooner, had sent any word as to her specific losses, the matter would have been looked into at once. As China has never had any ships that navigate in European waters, or in other seas included in the war zone, this solicitous reply was not without irony. I quote the reply:

To the Minister of Foreign Affairs of the Republic of China.

Your Excellency: By the instructions of my home government, which reached me at 7 P. M. on the 10th instant [March 10, 1917], I beg to forward you the following reply to China's protest to the latest blockade policy of Germany: The Imperial German Government expresses its great surprise at the threat used by the Government of the Republic of China in its note of protest. Many other countries have also protested, but China, which has been in friendly relations with Germany, is the only state which has added a threat to its protest. The surprise is doubly great because of the fact that as China has no shipping interests in the seas of blockaded zones, she will not suffer thereby.

The Government of the Republic of China mentions that loss of life of Chinese citizens has occurred as the result of the present method of war. The Imperial German Government wishes to point out that the Government of the Republic of China has never communicated with the Imperial Government regarding a single case of this kind, nor has it protested in this connection before. According to reports received by the Imperial Government, such losses as have been actually sustained by Chinese subjects have occurred in the firing line while they were engaged in digging trenches and other war service. While thus engaged, they were exposed to the dangers inevitable to all forces engaged in war. The fact that Germany has on several occasions protested against the employment of Chinese subjects for warlike purposes is evidence that the Imperial Government has given excellent proof of its friendly feelings towards China. In consideration of these friendly relations the Imperial Government is willing to treat the matter as if the threat had never been uttered. It is reasonable for the Imperial Government to expect that the Government of the Republic of China will revise its views respecting the question.

Germany's enemies were the first to declare a blockade on Germany, and the same is being persistently carried out. It is, therefore, difficult for Germany to cancel her blockade policy. The Imperial Government is nevertheless willing to comply with the wishes of the Government of China by opening negotiations to arrive at a plan for the protection of Chinese life and property, with the view that the end may be achieved and thereby utmost regard be given to the shipping rights of China. The reason which has prompted the Imperial Government to adopt this conciliatory policy is the knowledge that, once diplomatic relations are severed with Germany, China will not only lose a truly good friend, but will also be entangled in unthinkable difficulties.

In forwarding to Your Excellency the above instructions from my home Government, I also beg to state that, if the Government of China be willing, I am empowered to open negotiations for the protection of the shipping rights of China.

Imagine how disconcerting that reply must have been, since China has never had any ships in the war zone. Still less has she had any that have been or might possibly be sunk. With that excuse cut from under her, she is at present under the painful suspicion that this desire to uphold the sanctity of international law has been imposed from without. One is almost forced to the conclusion that it is imposed by those nations which themselves have been most flagrant violators of international law, upon Chinese territory. But be that as it may.

So much has been happening lately, that perhaps I have forgotten to mention a certain phase of international activity referred to in the German reply, that is, the employment of Chinese subjects behind the firing-lines in Europe. For a year past Chinese coolies have been recruited for service in France, paid of course, though probably not paid liberally, nor told frankly what they are being let in for. The French colonies have also been drafting their subjects for work in France. When we went down to the tropics in December, we traveled on a ship gathering coolies, mobilized not as soldiers but as laborers. The captain of our ship told us that up to date (December, 1916) France had already imported some forty thousand Annamites for work in munition factories, agricultural work, and noncombatant service behind the lines. The ship we were on was carrying some fourteen hundred of these little men, packed like sardines in the hold, which had been transformed into a sort of fifth-rate lodging-house, with tiers of bunks for the accommodation of these little coolies.

Each French ship of this particular line, going through the Mediterranean, carries between a thousand and fourteen hundred of such laborers; and what the effect of this will be upon the next generation of Frenchmen remains to be seen. They were pretty, docile little creatures, to be turned loose in villages and in the provinces, which villages and provinces have been bereft of men these many months, and where no race prejudice exists among the women. Many Frenchmen we have met deplored this state of things, and its probable effect upon the population of France. War is not very pretty, no matter from what angle you look at it. And now that the Chinese are being imported as well, the situation may become worse. An article entitled "China's Gift to the War in Human Labor and Human Life," has this to say:

Of far greater menace to Chinese interests [than the German submarine blockade] is the understanding which the Chinese Government is contemplating to make with France, Russia and Britain, for the despatch of laborers to Europe. The Chinese Government wants to indulge in coolie traffic. Bad business at any time, and worse now.

This business of sending Chinese laborers to these countries has been going on for over a year. It is done without regard to the interests of the people, or the wish of the Government. The companies for organizing the emigration were supposed to be under the inspiration of Mr. Liang-Shih-Yi, who was sure of making a few dollars on every coolie's head. The Chinese who have gone have been with Chinese cognizance, but not under Chinese protection. The business was of private or semi-official character, not of official character.

For several months English missionaries in the province of Shantung have been war-agents of the British Government for securing laborers for France and England. This has been done of late, at least, contrary to the wishes of the Chinese provincial authorities. Thus the English, like the Japanese in Shantung, have been going their own free way, without regard to the Chinese Government. The policy is bad missionary policy; the business is bad missionary business.

However, I ask myself—I who am nothing if not fair-minded—why should n't missionaries act as recruiting-agents? What 's the use of spending years converting heathen into Christians, if they are not to act as Christians? Why should there be any scruples about enlisting converts for a "Holy War"? They might as well "do their bit" for civilization, Christian civilization. Besides, "the blood of the martyrs is the seed of the Church." Moreover, the Treaty of Tientsin, in 1858, which legalized the sale of British opium, also legalized the practice of Christianity in China.[1]

[1] See Appendix II.

X

DUST AND GOSSIP

I DON'T suppose a country can go to war, without first having a war spirit. If the enemy does n't rouse this spirit, does n't provoke it, then some one else must. The ideal war, I suppose, is the one in which the enemy furnishes the incentive. Poor old China has now got to go to war, but it is mighty uphill work to create the war feeling. Since Germany has not provoked it, it must be manufactured somehow, and the task is now devolving upon those foreign influences which will benefit if China goes to war. They are getting to work rapidly and adroitly, but the situation requires some diplomacy. It is so difficult to incite feeling against one foreign nation without inciting it against them all. The poor Chinese can't distinguish. They can't understand why they should be especially irate against Germany at the moment, when rankling uppermost in their minds is the recent French grab of Lao Hsi Kai, and the still more recent deal of the Shanghai Opium Combine. It is so difficult to fan the flame yet not cause too great a conflagration. It requires nice discrimination, and these poor old heathen minds have a quaint logic of their own. The game is amusing, interesting, from the standpoint of the detached onlooker.

Roughly speaking, the people of a nation may be grouped into two classes, the inciters and the fighters. They are not the same people, as a rule. The inciters usually work in the rear, as noncombatants or molders of public opinion. In China—China being what it is, in the circumstances, and all—the noncombatants who have assumed this task of arousing the war spirit are foreigners. A delicate task, this arousing resentment against one set of foreigners without arousing it against all. It means diplomacy of the first water. Thus, the foreign press is very insistent that the Huns be got rid of. One English paper naïvely remarks: "We do not like to see Germans free to wander about our streets at will." Which is well enough in its way, although it must be galling to the Chinese to have outsiders refer to the streets of China as "ours." Americans would resent such a remark made by a foreigner concerning the streets of New York.

If only the European nations had been as decent to China as America has been! Then, in this crisis, China would have turned to them, been guided by them, with the same trust that she places in America. As it is, she distrusts all Europe to the core.

And over all this whirling dust of rumor and gossip, hatred and ill feeling, there has been raging for the past three days a physical dust-storm of tremendous intensity. The yellow, overhead kind,, sifting downward in clouds of powder, and covering everything, inside and out. The China-boys about the hotel tell us with superstitious awe that when a dust-storm lasts more than three days it is "bad joss." Such a storm, of a week's duration, preceded the outbreak of the Chinese-Japanese War.

Every one feels uneasy, the whole atmosphere is full of depression, tension, and suspense. One can't think or talk of anything but this impending disaster.

This afternoon we went out for a while to forget it, if we could. We went to the Lung Fu-Ssu, a sort of rag-fair held every ten days in the grounds of an old temple in the East City. It 's a wonderful fair, usually, with booths and stalls stretching in every direction, and spreading all over the ground, underfoot as well. Everything is sold at this bazaar, everything made in China or ever made in China, to-day or in the remote past,—porcelain, bronzes, jade, lacquer, silks, clothing, toys, fruits, food, curios, dogs and cats. Three times a month everything of every description finds its way to the Lung Fu-Ssu, and three times a month all foreign Peking, to say nothing of native Peking, finds its way to the temple grounds to look for bargains. To-day, however, it was n't much fun: neither the native city nor the legation quarter were out in force, for the dust was too thick, the air too cold.

Indefatigable bargain-hunters as we were, we could not stay long; but I don't believe it was because of the overwhelming dust; it was just sheer nervous anxiety to get back to the hotel for the latest news. We are all restless and anxious, and withal feel ourselves so utterly impotent to avert this impending calamity. Therefore, as I say, we did n't stay long at the fair,—just long enough for me to buy a pair of little, ancient, dilapidated stone lions, which the man assured me were of the Ming dynasty. My first venture into Ming. They looked it, anyway, when I bought them. I laid them at my feet in a newspaper, and—I suppose the jolting of the rickshaw did it—when we reached the hotel, the Ming had all rubbed off. They were stone lions of the purest plaster.

We found a note from the minister asking us in for tea, so we brushed ourselves hastily and went over to the legation to find a large crowd of dusty people assembled, in the beautiful, spacious drawing-rooms. Every one was talking politics, discussing the situation fore and aft, and, as usual, arriving nowhere. At the end of an hour there was a stir caused by the arrival of C——, one of the young, important Members of Parliament. He stood surrounded by an enquiring group, hands hidden up the capacious sleeves of his crackling brocade coat, while he sucked in his breath with hissing noises, in deference to the honorable company. "Good news!" he exclaimed, "good news! Or so I think you 'll find it! We have just decided to break with Germany!"

There was n't what you 'd call rejoicing; instead, his rather hilarious announcement was greeted with a sort of constrained silence. It 's such a tremendous thing for any country to declare war, and for a country in China's position it is such a blind leap into the abyss. However, the matter is not yet quite decided: the first vote is taken, but the final has yet to be cast. Parliament has been sitting all day. This, of course, merely means the severance of diplomatic relations, but the next step must follow as the night the day.

I must tell you of an incident that occurred the other day, when we were at tiffin at the home of some English acquaintances. But first I must tell you about the pailows, and before that again, I must tell you of the French ships that carry troops. I don't know where to begin, for you must hear everything if you are to see the point.

I 'll start with the pailows, those big, red lacquer memorial arches that span the streets all over the place—arch, by the way, being a figure of speech, since actually these arches are square, and consist of two upright posts with a third laid horizontally across them. They are emblazoned all over with gilded characters and sprawling dragons, and honor some great Chinese,—erected to his memory instead of a library or a hospital or something like that. Well, there is one pailow or memorial arch that is not of red lacquer but of white marble, erected not in honor of a Chinese but in honor of a foreigner, the imposing von Kettler Memorial which spans Ha-Ta-Men Street, far out. It is a Lest-We-Forget memorial placed in honor of Baron von Kettler, the German minister who was killed in the Boxer uprising. Chinese characters and German letters, carved in marble, tell the tale of von Kettler's death to all who pass beneath. Now to the ships. Three months ago when we went down to the tropics, we happened to travel on French ships, two of them loaded to the gunwales with troops for France, labor battalions. The passengers, I may mention, came off rather badly, being squeezed into exceedingly restricted quarters in order to make room for the troops. The first ship we were on carried a thousand, the other one twelve hundred of these little Annamites; the number varies according to the size of the vessel. Really, you know, I don't think it 's quite fair to either, to carry both troops and passengers on the same ship. Well, at tiffin to-day we heard what seemed like a most astounding proposal. Our host was explaining his plan for dealing with the von Kettler Memorial. The *Athos* was sunk

February 17, in the Mediterranean, together with five hundred Chinese soldiers. And here were we listening to a suggestion to erase the inscription on the von Kettler arch, and substitute a new one dedicating the pailow to the five hundred "Chinese" troops torpedoed by the Germans. It seems to me rather late in the day to begin inscribing pailows to Chinese killed by the conquering foreigner. To create the war spirit it may be necessary to dedicate the von Kettler pailow to this purpose, but as a precedent it seems rather unwise,—leads one into sweeping vistas of all the pailows of China, all the thousands innumerable of red lacquered pailows, all insufficient in their thousands to contain the names of the still greater thousands of Chinese slain by their European conquerors.

XI

DIPLOMATIC RELATIONS BROKEN

IT 'S done at last. China has at last broken diplomatic relations with Germany this fourteenth day of March, 1917. The foreign press is triumphant, while the Chinese press is much less enthusiastic, its rejoicings far less obvious. Here 's a bit of gossip for you, blown along with the dust of Peking. (By this time you must have discovered that Peking dust and Peking gossip are pretty much the same thing, whirling and blowing along together, sifting over you and into you, physically and mentally, till you are saturated through and through.) Miss Z—— told us this; she knows every bit of rumor in Peking, from topside down:

"What *do* you suppose happened, just two hours after the final vote was taken, and the note despatched to the German minister announcing China's decision? X—— [one of the Allied ministers] was seen ramping up and down before the German legation, shaking his fist at the German flag flying up above and shouting, 'That thing must come down! That thing must come down!' Had two Japanese soldiers with him, they say—where he got them heaven knows—but there he was, fairly raging, and stomping—that 's the word, stomping—up and down and shaking his fist at the flag, and shouting that it must come down!"

"Why did n't he wait till the Chinese took it down?"

"Lord only knows, my dear! Was n't it amusing! Could such things happen anywhere except in Peking?"

It appears, however, that while X—— was pacing up and down before the German legation, shaking his fist at the flag and furiously impatient at Chinese slowness, the wily Chinese were engaged upon other, more important matters. Hauling down the flag could wait; it was less urgent. The astute Chinese, with admirable foresight, hastily "acquired" the

German concessions in Tientsin and Hankow for themselves—acted with remarkable intelligence and great haste, almost undue haste, before any of the foreign powers could "acquire" or "protect" these concessions for themselves; put their own Chinese soldiers in possession, and with the utmost promptness occupied these German holdings in the name of the Republic of China. Imagine the shock! Furthermore, with the same speed, they also seized the interned German war-ships.

Well, this is a tremendous decision for China to have reached, and the next step, declaration of war, will be still more momentous. Opposition is growing all the while, in spite of the rupture of diplomatic relations, which does not mean that this country will declare war immediately, automatically, as a matter of course. Those in favor, and those who resist, are lining up for a tremendous struggle, and, as I wrote you before, some say that civil war will result.

One thing stands out clearly,—our whole visit to the East has confirmed it,—and that is that this European war had its origin in the

Orient. Supremacy in the Orient, control of the Far East—that is the underlying cause of the struggle which is rending Europe in twain. The world does not go to war for little stakes, for trifles. It fights for colossal stakes, worth gambling for.

XII

WALKING ON THE WALL

DON'T think that even in all this excitement our taste for shopping has become quiescent. Far from it! Shopping freshens one up, relaxes one's mind, makes one more keen for the next bit of rumor that comes along. We know where all the antique-shops are situated, those along Ha-ta-Men Street, out on Morrison Street, in the Tartar City, all those without the Wall, and those in the Chinese City, as well as the pawnshops down the lower part of Chi'en Men Street, the Thieves' Market, and all the various bazaars. And we know the days on which the temple fairs are held. We know all about them and get bargains every day, sometimes real finds, and sometimes stone lions of the purest Ming, such as I described a few days ago. And in the intervals, when we are not out questing on our own, the dealers and runners from the various shops appear at our door, bow themselves in with such ingratiating compliments that we can't resist, and then stoop over and undo wonderful blue cotton bundles and exhibit such treasures that there 's no withstanding them. The most irresistible of all these dealers is "Tiffany" (his Chinese name has given way to this nickname, which is solemnly printed on his card), dealer in jewels and jade, a giant Chinese about six feet tall, weighing some three hundred pounds, with the smiling, innocent face of a three-foot child! When Tiffany enters the room and squats down over his big blue bundle, his knees spread out, he looks like a wide blue elephant, and there is no refusing his bland, smiling, upturned face, his gentle, "No buy. Just look-see." Then from the bundle come strings of pearls, translucent jade of "number-one" quality, snuff-bottles fit for a museum. The only way of getting rid of him is to tell him that a new American lady has just arrived on the floor below, whereupon he gathers up his treasures and goes in search of her! His method of gaining admittance to our room is ingenious. A gentle knock, and we open to find the doorway suffused by Tiffany.

"No want things to-day, Mr. Tiffany. No can buy."

To which comes the pleasant reply: "No want Missy buy. Come bring Missy cumshaw."

A slender hand slips around the open door, against one side of which I press my knee while he braces a huge foot against the other, and in the hand lies a red leather box painted with flowers and dragons. "Present for Missy; cumshaw," says the pleasant voice, and what can you do? "Amelican lady you say down-stair, she buy heap pearls, so I bring Missy cumshaw." Whereupon in he comes, with his gratitude for the American lady, his bargains, his wheedling, and we are lost!

After some weeks of this—Tiffany and others, and our own excursions—our room became a veritable curio-shop, and our curios were so overlaid with spring dust which the

Village outside walls of Peking.

Fortune teller

"boys" had failed to remove that we called in a packer one day, had everything boxed, and resolved to buy nothing more. On this afternoon, March 16, we went over to the legation compound to arrange with our consul for invoices, and as we crossed the compound Dr. Reinsch appeared from his house, and came over and spoke to us. He looked very tired and troubled, showing the strain of the last few weeks.

"I 've just had word from the Chinese Foreign Office," he said, "that the Russian Government has been overturned!" He had no details, just the mere fact, but the shock was so great that we forgot all about our visit to the consul, forgot our intention to obtain an invoice; all we wanted to do was get off and talk it over! We flew back to the hotel, simply bursting with the news! It 's so exciting, in this old, barbaric city, to hear such news as that, so casually, from your minister! No one in the hotel to talk to,—three o'clock, a bad hour! So we went for a walk on the only available place for a walk that Peking affords, the top of the wall. For you can't walk with comfort in the streets, they are too crowded, with camels and wheelbarrows to be dodged at every turn. And as we walked on the wall, discussing that bit of tremendous news, going over and over again the possibilities contained in those few words, we met other people out walking, also talking it over. The French minister and his first-secretary came by, deeply engrossed in conversation. Some little distance behind us came Dr. Reinsch with one of the press correspondents. We met all diplomatic Peking walking on the wall that afternoon, talking it over! For the wall is a good safe place for conversations: one can't possibly be overheard, for one can see people coming a mile off. Only foreigners may go there: the Chinese are n't allowed on it, except the soldiers at the blockhouses by the towers. The most frequent visitor is the baby camel owned by the American marine guards, which comes up to browse on the weeds growing between the stones. We once asked a marine where they found this mascot. "Stole it first," was the reply, "and paid four dollars afterward!"

I picked up a Tientsin paper a few days ago, and was interested to read an "Ordonnance" promulgated by the French consul-general at Tientsin. By the terms of this decree every Chinese employed in the French concession is obliged to have a little book containing his name, age, place of birth, and so on, together with his photograph and finger-prints. A duplicate *carnet* is on file at the French police bureau in Tientsin, and no Chinese can find employment in the concession, as cook, groom, clerk, chauffeur, or in any other capacity, unless he is first registered with the police. The idea of having one's finger-prints recorded, like a common criminal, seems somehow humiliating. I imagine there would be some comment if the Japanese enforced such regulations in their concessions in China.

XIII

MEETING THE PRESIDENT OF CHINA

EVER since we came to Peking we have been anxious to meet the President of China, Li Yuan Hung. Dr. Reinsch said he would arrange it for us "at the first opportune moment." Opportune moments are scarce in Peking, as you can well imagine; consequently we have been waiting for weeks for such a moment to arrive, for a pause longer than usual between impeachments and betrayals and plots of various kinds. We had waited so long, in fact, that we had quite forgotten about it, until we came in one day just before tiffin time, rather late, and found the whole hotel in a blaze of excitement: we were to meet the President that afternoon!

And, what 's more, best clothes were required! Really, I had not foreseen that contingency, and therefore felt uncomfortable and self-conscious when arrayed in my other hat, with the feather, the hat which has been reposing in the hat-box for eight long months, waiting for just such an emergency! Every one else, however, was in the same state of excitement as to dress; that is, all those who like ourselves had been long in the Orient, and whose clothes had fallen off a bit in appearance. In sharp contrast were the newly arrived tourists with their smart new outfits, beautiful as only Americans can be beautiful. But never mind: we reflected that the President would never know the difference; he would consider us all alike and all outlandish. There were others in the party who had lived so long in Peking that they were reduced to Gillard's best,—Gillard's, the one "department store" of the city, about on a plane with the general store of a country village or a frontier town, only worse. Sooner or later every one in Peking is reduced to Gillard's Emporium, where the stocks are old-fashioned and musty, and the thing you want has just been sold out. And if you can't get it at Gillard's, there is nowhere else to go. Up-stairs Mrs. Gillard makes Paris gowns on the latest models, which look all right, too, till tourist season comes round and you see the difference. Well, finally we were all ready, and assembled at the front door of the hotel,—the smart and beautiful Americans; those clad in Gillard's best, and ourselves, something intermediate. The men were upset, too: several of them had been obliged to borrow top hats. And at the last moment a rumor spread that ceremonial bows were required. That created such consternation that several of us considered backing out.

We were all to meet at the Pei Hei Gate at two o'clock, so we started early, for we had a long distance to travel. The smart Americans went in motors, as was fitting, but the rest of us made a long procession of rickshaws, and jogged happily along the dusty streets, out through the gates of the legation quarter, past the North Glacis, through the gates of the Imperial City, and finally, after half an hour's run, reached the Pei Hei Gate, leading into the old and abandoned Winter Palace.

It then transpired that a visit to this old palace was part of the program, and we were to wander for two hours through its beautiful and extensive grounds, until four o'clock, when the President would receive us. Now March is March the world over, but March in Peking is excessive. No one who has not passed a spring in North China can know the meaning of dust. On this clear, bright March afternoon a classic dust-storm was in progress and in this, dressed in our best clothes, we were to wander for two hours through the closed grounds of the Winter Palace, which had been thrown open to us by special courtesy of the President!

They say one never realizes the meaning of the word decay until one has seen Peking. And the climax of decay is reached here, in this former abode of the old empress dowager, where everything remains as she left it, or as the Boxers left it, or as the European looters left it after the Boxer troubles. Scattered through the beautiful grounds are magnificent buildings, all fallen into ruin. The roofs of the palaces and temples, blazing with the imperial yellow tiles, are dropping to pieces, and rank grass is replacing the fallen tiles and dislodging those that are left. In one of the temples we walked through littered débris of rich carvings, kicked against the broken heads and hands of gilded gods fallen from the altars, and brushed against the loosened shreds of old paintings swaying in tatters from the walls. One building contained the remains of a once beautiful fountain, painted and lacquered, now moldering and fallen into dust. At the four corners of the room the old gods, life-size, had been gathered into piles and covered with matting, and from beneath this dusty covering protruded dirty, battered heads and gilded bodies, ludicrous and pathetic.

In the grounds it was no better. Weeds grew shoulder high, springing from between the stones of the great courtyards and open spaces connecting the temples and palaces, and we pushed ourselves through this brush, and stumbled over rolling stones, all the while enveloped by the whirling dust, the everlasting

Peking dust, straight from the Gobi Desert. All this was very disastrous to our personal appearance, and at the end of two hours we were all reduced to pretty much the same level: really, there was n't much difference between the beautiful Americans, those attired in Gillard's best, and ourselves, when we took to our rickshaws (and motors) again and set off for the President's palace, in the Forbidden City.

The grounds of this palace presented a much better appearance than anything we had seen in Peking. The roads were newly swept, and everything was very neat and clean and orderly, though bare. The lawns, if such they could be called, were as arid and grassless as the great plains of Chili. We arrived a few minutes before four, and descended from our vehicles, grand and otherwise, and then a cleaning-up process took place. Dusty shoes were brushed off with handkerchiefs, dusty coats slapped and patted, wind-blown hair rearranged, dust cleaned out from the corners of eyes, and powder-papers passed from hand to hand among the women. One lady remarked cheerfully, "Well, we surely don't look very nifty to meet the President," but we made ourselves as "nifty" as we could, in the circumstances, standing together in a laughing group on the lee side of the palace, and asking one another if we 'd do. I remember that once, years ago, when I was living in the Latin Quarter, some of us went over to a tea on "the other side," and before pulling the door-bell, we stood first on one foot and then on the other, polishing our dusty shoes on our stockings. Well, here we were doing the same thing, before meeting the President of China!

We got clean at last, and then soberly marched round the corner of the building and presented ourselves in the anteroom of the palace, leading to the President's apartments. Here we found Dr. Reinsch waiting for us, and he sorted us into groups of eight, and left us waiting till the summons came. In former times the mandarins used to wait in this anteroom, before an audience with the empress dowager, and we tried to imagine the big bare room of to-day filled with these high officials in their gorgeous robes. Nothing remains of the old glories of the palace save the elaborate carving on wall and ceiling, and a few pieces of magnificent old furniture. The ceiling is now disfigured with a gaudy, cheap European chandelier, while standing here and there on beautiful ebony tables are hideous modern vases, straight from the five-and-ten-cent store. The floor was covered with ugly oil-cloth. Such is China modernized, imbued with Western culture.

Our group of eight was the first to be called, and Dr. Reinsch led the way with an interpreter. We passed out of the antechamber and along an open marble corridor, lined with Chinese soldiers in their padded gray cotton uniforms, who stood at salute as the American minister passed. Immediately we found ourselves in another room, also plainly furnished, and the next moment were shaking hands with an unassuming little man clad in a frock-coat, the President, Li Yuan Hung. Through the interpreter the President explained that he would like us to pass into the room beyond, where he could speak with us one by one, personally. He waved his hand toward the other room, and my recollection is that we led the way! It all happened so quickly, I can't remember; but somehow our group seemed to be waiting in the other room when the President and Dr. Reinsch arrived at our heels, a second later. However, you can't expect people not brought up in courts to know much about such things, and we were probably flustered, anyway.

President Li, Dr. Reinsch, and the interpreter stood together, while we arranged ourselves in a semicircle round them, and then Dr. Reinsch presented each one of us in turn, explained who each one was, or what he or she represented or had been doing. He began with the Allens,—told who Mr. Allen was, what big American interests he represented, why he had come out to China, and all about it. Then the interpreter repeated all this to the President, who meanwhile stood looking inquiringly at the Allens, as did the rest of us. When the translation was finished, Li

Courtesy of Press Illustrating Service

President Li Yuan-Hung

Entrance to Winter Palace

replied in Chinese; they say he can speak English, but imperfectly, and he did not attempt it. "When quality meets, compliments pass." Dr. Reinsch said all manner of nice things about the Allens and China, and the President said all sorts of nice things about the Allens and America, and it all took some time, just disposing of the first two of our party. Meanwhile, two servants came in with a tray of champagne and plates of cakes, and we all stood with a glass in one hand and a cake in the other, waiting to see what Mr. Allen would do when the President finished telling him how glad he was he had come to China. Mr. Allen rose to it, however, in a happy little speech, saying that it was a privilege, and so on.

Then came our turn. We were anxiously wondering what Dr. Reinsch could find to say about us two, having committed himself by introducing the whole group at one swoop as "representative Americans." However, we were both exceedingly pleased at what he did say, and the President was pleased, too, apparently, for he replied that he was glad we were like that. So it continued all round the circle, and we felt exactly as if it were the Day of Judgment, and the secrets of all hearts were being revealed: we thought we knew our friends pretty well, and all about them; yet we hung with bated breath upon Dr. Reinsch's introduction or send-off! And we had never understood the meaning of "true Oriental politeness" until we heard the President's gracious, courteous welcome in reply. We stood directly opposite him, and had a good opportunity to observe him closely,—a short, thick-set man with a small mustache, much darker than the usual Chinese type, owing to his heritage of Siamese blood. Many people say he has no Siamese blood at all, but it is always like that in China: whatever any one tells you is always flatly contradicted by the next person you meet.

Then we committed a great *gaffe!* When the Allens and E—— and I had been safely disposed of, and the introductions and interpretations were being directed toward the other four members of the party, we drank our champagne—we four, the Allens and ourselves! I think it was because we did not know what else to do with it, having stood stiffly at attention for some twenty minutes, trying to balance a very full glass in one hand, and conscious that the sugary cake in the other was fast melting. Anyway, we emptied our glasses, and set them down on a table behind us, and ate the cakes as well. Then, to our horror, Dr. Reinsch summed us all up again, collectively, in a graceful little speech, and the President raised his glass, and bowing, drank our health. I heard E—— whisper, "The glasses, quick!" and the Allens and she and I hastily groped backward for the empty glasses on the table behind us, and drained the few remaining drops with what manners we could muster. After which we all shook hands with the President again, and filed out of the room.

In the anteroom the rest of the party crowded round us, asking for tips. We had two big ones to offer: *Don't* lead the way for the President of China, and don't touch your glasses till he raises his!

XIV

GREAT BRITAIN'S TWELVE DEMANDS

THE scaffolding is being put up for more trouble. China has got to declare war, and to do it soon. It took five weeks' manœuvering to make her break diplomatic relations and will probably take much longer to induce her to take this next step, opposition to which is growing stronger and more intense every day. The President is obstinately opposed to it, and he has considerable backing. There is free talk about a revolution occurring if the break takes place, so determined are certain leaders not to be dominated by "foreign influence." Many Chinese can be bribed, but the Chinese in general cannot be fooled, and no glowing compliments about China's "masculine" attitude can deceive them as to the yoke they must wear should they decide to surrender themselves and place their nation at the disposal of European interests.

On the morning of March 26 one of the papers contained this significant article, under the caption of Tibetan Affairs:

Reported British Demands. Indignation of Chinese M. P.'s. Mr. Ho Sheng-Ping and other Senators have addressed the following interpellation to the Government: "According to the reports of the Japanese newspapers, the British Government has sent Twelve Demands to the Chinese Government in connection with Tibetan affairs, and these demands, being so cruel and unreasonable, tend to provoke the anger and indignation of any people. Why did we address a protest to the German Government against its submarine warfare? And why did we declare diplomatic severance with Germany? Was it not to render assistance to the Entente Powers, and was it not to render direct help to Great Britain? We are, indeed, surprised at these British Demands appearing in the newspapers. In accordance with the provisions laid down in Article 19 of the Provisional Constitution, we hereby demand that a reply be given within five days as to the true nature of the reported Demands, and the attitude of the Government towards them."

The Demands from Great Britain as reported in the Japanese newspapers are as follows:

1 Great Britain shall have the right to construct railways between India and Tibet.
2 The Chinese Government shall contract loans from the British Government for the improvement of the administration of Tibet.
3 The treaty obligations between Tibet and Great Britain shall be considered valid as heretofore.
4 British experts shall be engaged for the industrial enterprises of Tibet.
5 China shall secure the redemption of loans contracted from the British people by the Tibetans.
6 Neither China nor Great Britain shall send troops to Tibet without reason.
7 The Chinese Government shall not appoint or dismiss officials in Tibet on its own responsibility.
8 The British Government shall be allowed to establish telegraph lines in Lhassa, Chiangchu, Chamutao, etc.
9 British postal service shall be introduced in Lhassa and other places.
10 China shall not interfere with the actions of the British Government in Tibet.
11 No privileges or interests in Tibet shall be granted to other nations.
12 All mines in Tibet shall be jointly worked by the British and Chinese Governments.

These Twelve Demands, which the Chinese

M. P.'s resent so hotly, which they quaintly term "cruel and unreasonable," virtually amount to the annexation of Tibet by the British Government. It is amusing to think that it was the Japanese press which first gave them publicity. We are so accustomed to hearing of the famous Twenty-one Demands of Japan that we fail to realize that other nations make demands equally sweeping and equally arbitrary. Of course, these British demands will not receive the world-wide attention accorded those of Japan. Remember, over here it is not customary to think of or speak of anything but "Japanese aggression." Japan, you see, offers the only stumbling-block to the complete domination of the Orient by Europe. But for Japan—China might possibly become another India. And the Japanese, facing race discrimination and exclusion from most of the European countries, and many of their colonies, as well as America, cannot afford to have China under European control. It is a question of self-preservation.

We were dining the other evening with a Chinese gentleman, of high position, who invited us to dinner at an old and very famous restaurant outside the palace gates. It was at this restaurant, in the days of the dowager empress, that the Mandarins used to assemble every night while waiting for the imperial edicts to be issued from the palace. And as the edicts frequently did not appear until two or three in the morning, they comforted themselves, during this long wait, with much fine and delicate food cooked in the fine and delicate manner that even French cooks cannot excel. And if the cooking in those days was as delicious as at present, they passed the time very pleasantly, and did very well by themselves, those old officials.

It was a bitterly cold night, and the dark street in front of the restaurant was crowded with a motley array of rickshaws, Peking carts, and motors, through which we made our way by the light of a bobbing lantern. We entered a crowded, noisy kitchen, filled with rushing waiters and shouting cooks bending over charcoal fires. In contrast to the freezing wind outside the air was deliciously warm, redolent with the fumes of charcoal and the aroma of savory exotic food. Our table was waiting for us in a private dining-room; the whole place consists of private dining-rooms, separated by good thick stone walls, so that one can't hear the plots and intrigues being hatched next door, though the din in the open courtyard caused by the scrambling, yelling waiters would make that impossible, in any event. The room had a stone floor, and was unheated, only a little less cold than outdoors. Inadvertently, we took off our wraps,—not all, only two or three; for we are becoming quite Chinese in our manner of putting one coat on over another. We put them all on again, however, at the end of the second course, for the draughty windows and the door constantly swinging open into the courtyard made all our warm things indispensable.

Our Chinese gentleman gave us a "number-one" dinner, and a number-one dinner always begins with bird's-nest soup, the greatest delicacy a Chinese can offer; also, the most expensive. Well, we began with it, and truly it is "number-one"—gelatinous, delicate, with an exquisite flavor altogether indescribable. Then followed the other courses. As this dinner was given to foreigners, we had only twelve courses, whereas the usual Chinese dinners run up into the dozens; "forty curses" they are sometimes called by unwary foreigners who have tried to eat their way through a whole meal. The courses come on and on, endlessly; but the proper Chinese custom is that you leave when you have had enough, say four or five. You are n't supposed to sit through an entire meal. Our host told us that he had been to three dinners that evening, before this one, and was expecting to go to one or two more. We felt rather uneasy when he told us this, and thought we ought to be going, ourselves; but he hastily explained that this dinner, given in our honor, was not long and that we must go through all of it. Very easy going, I must say!

After the bird's-nest soup came shark fins,

another delicacy and also delicious. Then fish, then soup of another kind, then powdered chicken, then duck and rice, then cake, then shell-fish, then more duck, then lotus-flower soup, and finally fruit and coffee. As each wonderful dish succeeded the other our host apologized profusely, deprecating its poor quality and miserable manner of preparation. We protested vehemently, with enthusiasm. This also is Chinese etiquette, it seems, for the host to denounce each dish, while the guests eat themselves to a standstill. It all took a long time, for we managed our chop-sticks badly; nevertheless, in spite of this handicap, we finished every marvelous course placed before us. A tea-pot of hot sake did something to kccp the creeping chill out of our bones, but very little: the thimble-like sake cups contained only a few drops, and one does n't like to ask for the tea-pot more than seventeen times! During the meal Mr. Y—— entertained us with many side-lights on the political situation, and we finally asked him to explain the meaning of the Twelve British

Demands. He replied promptly, emphatically.

"They are a threat," he said, "a form of coercion, to make us take the next step, to declare war. If we declare war, they will be withdrawn. We are familiar with them. They have appeared before, when it was necessary."

XV

CONCLUSION

ON the first of April we are going to leave Peking, to leave China alone to her fate! We have had enough of it, and are just about worn out with the strain on our sympathies. Opposition to a declaration of war is growing daily, and so are rumors of a revolution. But a revolution is just what is needed,—a revolution which will unseat those who are opposed to the war, and which will place in power a group of officials submissive and subservient to European influence. A revolution will offer the grand, final excuse for the "protection" of China, by Europe. You will see; mark my words. Only, of course, Japan will not be the power that sets in order this disturbed country. Never Japan, the great commercial competitor. For by this time you must surely understand that Japanese aggression is immoral and reprehensible, whereas European aggression or "civilization" is the fate to which the Orient is predestined. The world contains a double standard of international justice, for the East and the West.

At least we are glad to have been in China during these distressful days, just to see how they do it. With the attention of the world centered on Europe, things are taking place out here which could not possibly occur were the world free to know of them, and judge. But in the safe seclusion of Oriental isolation all things are now possible. Back of the war, behind the war, ugly things are going on, which will be all finished and done with and safely accomplished by the time the war is over. This war for civilization is all that "civilization" requires in the way of opportunity in the Orient.

So we are going to leave Peking, gorgeous, barbaric Peking, with its whirling clouds of gossip and its whirling clouds of dust. We are stifled by them both. We are going to Japan to see cherry-blossoms.

APPENDIXES

APPENDIX I

This despatch appeared in "The New York Times," the last of July or the first part of August, 1918:

FEAR OPIUM TRADE REVIVAL IN CHINA

British Protest Lodged Against Large Tract of Poppy Under Cultivation in Shensi. Government is Helpless. Area is Practically Ruled by Bandits. May Try to Enforce the Law.

From a Special Correspondent. Peking, May 27, 1918:

One of the very few things which China has done well is the suppression of the opium practice with all its baneful influences. Under the spur of enlightened foreign opinion, the Chinese have rid themselves of opium much earlier than was arranged for, and in their thoroughness actually defied conventions to which the British Government was a party.

This in other circumstances might have awkward consequences. But those who took the risk knew that the British people would not tolerate the continuance of opium importation into China even if it did involve the violation of certain agreements.

For several years now China has been certified as free, that is to say, the cultivation of the poppy has been entirely discontinued. Of course the habit has not been completely eliminated—that takes time—and the fact that a demand for the drug exists is sufficient temptation for greedy officials and unscrupulous speculators to connive at renewed attempts to cultivate the poppy and resume its sale and use.

The state of lawlessness which prevails in China invites disregard of authority, especially when it affords lucrative possibilities, and the continued enfeeblement of the administration in Peking contributes to conditions favoring the resumption of the traffic in opium.

It is not surprising, therefore, to learn that reports have been received by the British Legation in Peking, of large tracts being under poppy cultivation in Shensi, a province where lawlessness is rampant, and where the unfortunate residents are harassed, plundered and murdered by large roving bands of Tufei, the Chinese equivalent for robbers or thieves. The reports come from missionaries and foreign travellers and naturally they could not be ignored.

Accordingly, the British Minister has lodged a protest with the Chinese Government. *Under the Opium Convention, Indian opium may be imported into China as long as the poppy is cultivated in China. That is the legal aspect,* but in these days of higher ideals, it may be presumed that Sir John Jordan and the British Government, which he represents, are more concerned with the moral aspect. *His protest is not made in the interests of Indian opium,* but in the hope that the national regeneration from a former vice should not suffer a relapse.

The reply of the Chinese Government is not known, but it is safe to infer that assurance would be given that orders would be issued to the provincial authorities to enforce the law prohibiting the cultivation of the poppy. Whether these orders will be obeyed is not so certain.

Gone are the days when edicts from Peking concluded with the warning, "tremble and obey." Then they were heeded, but now the authority of the Government does not seem to extend beyond the metropolitan area, and however ready the administration may be to suppress poppy cultivation, it is unable to control the more distant feudal tuchuns. How then, can a Government be held responsible when it is not in a position to enforce its authority? This problem meets the treaty powers at every turn. One or several must act as did Alexander the Great when he cut the Gordian knot. Who or which shall it be?

From an article in the "North China Herald," dated September 14, 1918:

The Government [Chinese] after concluding the opium deal, farmed the right to sell the drug in Chekiang, Hupeh and Kiangsu, to a specially formed company, called the Hsichi Company.

We read further in the article that the Hsichi Company bought opium from the Chinese Government at the rate of 10,000 taels per chest, which it sells to district farmers at 23,000 taels per chest, and these latter retail it to drug-stores or consumers at 27,000 taels per chest.

From Millard's "Review of the Far East," October 12, 1918:

It would be advisable for the Peking government to seriously consider the notes addressed to it on the subject of opium by the British and American governments. The trade in opium cannot any more be successfully revived in China than could the African slave trade, and if Peking proposes to make a few dollars by the sale of the over-plus opium stock at Shanghai the venture is dangerous. Only a few years ago China gave her pledge, in the presence of the assembled nations at The Hague, that the poppy plant should never again be cultivated within her borders, nor would the traffic in opium be tolerated, and in the notes from the British and American governments the pledge given at The Hague is brought directly to the attention of those in authority at Peking. The two Western governments named would hardly have taken such concurrent action without a significant meaning, and a meaning which Peking will not be permitted to treat with indifference and impunity. It is certainly not the policy of either British or American governments to interfere in the domestic affairs of China, but both of those governments do intend that no business shall be carried on as demoralizing and offensive to the moral sense of the world as the business of debauching and drugging with opium. London and Washington really do not appear to be fully enlightened as to conditions at Peking and the motives and inspirations influencing officials in that Capital, and a reformation there is as much needed as in Russia. It may be written that at no time in Chinese history, during the past two hundred years, has the name of China been so disparaged and her reputation besmirched. Representatives of the Allied nations and America are in Russia charged with the duty of aiding in bringing about the unity of the Russian people that they may establish a stable government, and representatives of a similar character for a like purpose are as much needed in China. Russia will soon have a stable government, the choice of her people, but China promises to go on unsettled so long as Peking governs as at present.

From the "New York Times," November 25, 1918:

CHINA TO DESTROY OPIUM

1,200 CHESTS TO BE BURNED IN DEFERENCE TO ALLIED REPRESENTATIONS

Copyright, 1918, by The New York Times Company.
Special Cable to "The New York Times."

PEKING, Nov. 23.—The Government has decided to destroy the remaining stocks of opium in Shanghai in deference to Anglo-American representations. Three hundred chests have been sold, and 1,200 will be burned in presence of the allied representatives, the Government making a virtue of necessity.

America to the rescue! It must have been a close squeak for poor old China.

APPENDIX II

From the "New York Medical Record," October 12, 1918:

THE ORIGIN OF THE SO-CALLED "SPANISH INFLUENZA"

By James Joseph King, A.B., M.D.
NEW YORK
CAPTAIN MEDICAL CORPS, U. S. ARMY

We desire to present in this preliminary note a consideration of the similarity of the present epidemic to the epidemic of pneumonic plague which broke out in Harbin, China, in October, 1910, and spread rapidly and continuously throughout Northern China at that time; and to suggest that this epidemic may be the same disease modified by racial and topographical differences. The origin of this epidemic was suggested to the writer soon after its outbreak in our camps by Mr. Guy M. Walker, an eminent American authority on Chinese affairs. This suggestion led to an investigation of the reports of the pneumonic plague in China and there is sufficient likeness of that epidemic to the present one prevailing in our cities and army camps to warrant a consideration of it.

In the latter part of 1910 the pneumonic plague first appeared in Harbin a town in Manchuria under Chinese control. Harbin is on the Trans-Siberian Railroad, and was the original hotbed of the disease. The plague had prevailed in Russia previous to November, 1910, but the Russians, alert to its danger, took immediate action and stamped it out. It was believed that the plague was carried into Harbin by the fur dealers and by the Chinese laborers returning to their homes to celebrate New Year's Day, a custom universally observed in China. From Harbin the plague rapidly spread in all directions, usually following the lines of traffic along the railroads. It spread as far south as Chefu, a seaport town, probably having been carried there by Chinese coolies returning from the north.

. . . .

This plague has been very serious The mortality has been fearfully high. It has spread throughout China. Wherever the Chinese coolies from the North have traveled they have carried this disease. From 1910 up to 1917 China has not been free from it. The writer has heard of several cases being present in Peking last year.

In the early part of 1917, about 200,000 Chinese coolies, collected from the northern part of China, where the pneumonic plague has raged at intervals since 1910, were sent to France as laborers. Part of them were sent around through the Mediterranean; some, perhaps the majority, were sent across the Pacific, and then through Canada and America, to be transported across the Atlantic to France. Trainloads of these coolies were sent in solid trains across the United States to New York and thence to France. They made splendid laborers in France, and were in back of the lines during the German drive of March, 1918. No doubt many of them were captured by the Germans at that time. Hence the outbreak of it in the German army and its rapid spread in Spain.

So far as we know, this disease first broke out last spring, in the German army, where it is said to have been very serious. We next heard of it in Spain, hence the name Spanish influenza. The name is really a misnomer, but it has stuck probably because it is the first epidemic of influenza that Spain has ever had. Since our soldiers and sailors have been returning from the battlefields of France it has become very prevalent and serious in our camps and cities all over this country.

. . . .

. . . It seems possible that the *Bacillus pestis* may have been present in a non-virulent state in the Chinese coolies, and assumed new virulence, vigor, and a somewhat different form, when transplanted into virgin soil. The high mortality and infectivity of this epidemic strongly suggest it.

On this basis the epidemics which have followed all great wars may be explained. If a nation or tribe can survive any disease long enough it will acquire immunity to that disease. When, however, foreign people commingle freely and intimately, as in war, epidemics will break out. The inactive, non-virulent organisms in one race will become virulent in some other race which has not acquired immunity to that specific organism.